THE PARLIAMENTARIAN OF TOMORROW

THE PARLIAMENTARIAN OF TOMORROW

A Practical Guide for Those Entering the Profession and Practicing Professionals Adjusting to a Changing Environment

Gene Bierbaum, PhD

Certified Professional Parliamentarian
American Institute of Parliamentarians®

Professional Registered Parliamentarian
National Association of Parliamentarians®

To order additional copies of this book, contact:
Xlibris Corporation
1-888-795-4274
www.Xlibris.com
Orders@Xlibris.com
82028

CONTENTS

Chapter

Appendix

To my wife Agnes,
my 24/7 editor-in-chief,
who inspired me to write.
Also,
the Lester L. Dahms Memorial Foundation
keeping his memory alive
and strengthening the profession
that he served with distinction.

FOREWORD

I am deeply honored to have been invited to write this foreword for Dr. Bierbaum's new book on the parliamentary profession. Dr. Bierbaum has been a mainstay of the profession for the past thirty-five years, and I can think of no one better qualified for such an undertaking.

My first contacts with Dr. Bierbaum were as a student attending AIP practicums and the teacher education course. I will never forget his participatory workshops in which he gently led his students through the stages of learning. He has the "magic touch" that enables him to bring out the best in his students. He gave us the courage to try new approaches and to learn from our mistakes without fear of negative criticism or embarrassment.

Dr. Bierbaum's teaching legacy continues today through the annual workshops offered by the Lester L. Dahms Memorial Foundation as well as through NAP and AIP workshops. His active involvement in these organizations continues, and the profession is indebted to him for this book and for his many contributions to the education and preparation of future parliamentarians.

Ronald Stinson, President
National Association of Parliamentarians®

FOREWORD

Reading through Dr. Bierbaum's latest publication, I was struck by his in-depth understanding of our profession and where it is headed. The building blocks described by Dr. Bierbaum lay a clear foundation for any professional wishing to become a knowledgeable and successful parliamentarian in today's world. The path outlined by Dr. Bierbaum can provide clients with the security and peace of mind that comes from hiring someone who is fully prepared and well rounded.

Dr. Bierbaum has performed many valuable services for AIP since he first joined in 1972, serving as president, accrediting director, education director, annual session coordinator, ethics chairman, founder of the teacher certification course, and curriculum director of the AIP practicums. Of all the hats he has worn, however, Dr. Bierbaum will be best remembered as a teacher. Teaching is his passion, and his students, among whom I include myself, will always be grateful for his gentle, patient guidance in the classroom.

Dr. Bierbaum's teaching skills are again on display in this book. Here he explains and clarifies the intricacies of the parliamentary profession in terms that anyone can understand and appreciate. Mindful of the past and always with an eye toward the future, Dr. Bierbaum traces the growth of the profession and demonstrates how it still has much more room to grow. I view this book as a must read for both aspiring and experienced parliamentarians.

James N. Jones, President
American Institute of Parliamentarians®

PREFACE

I have long been aware that professional parliamentarians are not the same. No advanced degree is required to enter the profession, nor are the members licensed. Coming from many different disciplines with sharply different backgrounds of educational achievement, parliamentarians appear in many stripes and colors and practice their profession very differently. Yet as this book will show, parliamentarians do have certain common denominators that bring them together as members of a profession.

Much has been written about parliamentary procedure, but little has been written about the profession as a whole. The purpose of this book is to explore and describe the key attributes of the parliamentary profession. What are the building blocks that comprise its foundation? How have these building blocks interacted to produce The Parliamentarian of Today, and what trends do they reveal that will shape The Parliamentarian of Tomorrow?

This book is written for anyone wishing to learn about what a parliamentarian is and for client organizations wishing to learn more about what a parliamentarian does. Aspiring parliamentarians, as well as seasoned professionals will gain a better understanding of the profession and how they can adjust to accommodate the future demands of client organizations. My hope for all readers is that you will acquire an understanding of the composition and status of today's profession, how it arrived at its present stage of development, and how it is likely to evolve in the future.

I am deeply indebted to those who assisted me, especially my wife Agnes who inspired me to write and remained constantly at my side, encouraging me every step of the way. Jean Babcock, Coleen Duris, and Betty Green provided valuable assistance in editing the manuscript. Also, I am grateful to Jack Osgard, a good friend and accomplished bridge player, who volunteered to help provide the finishing touches.

Finally, I wish to thank the Lester L. Dahms Memorial Foundation for its foresight and leadership in promoting the parliamentary profession as a whole. Since its inception, the foundation has reached out to all parliamentarians regardless of their organizational affiliation or level of expertise. Cleon Babcock, Ardis Dahms, and Jeanette Williams are prominent among those who have promoted the annual workshops since 1993, and I am fortunate to count these among my best friends. I am especially grateful to the foundation for its continued efforts to honor the memory of one of the profession's most dedicated and talented leaders, Lester L. Dahms.

CHAPTER ONE

The Parliamentary Profession Defined

Much has been written about parliamentarians and the work that they do for client organizations, but little has been written about the profession as a whole. What, exactly, is this mysterious profession? Who are its members, and what characteristics do they share in common? To answer these questions, we will first look at the common, everyday means by which most people get involved in parliamentary procedure; then we shall examine the stages through which they evolve; and finally, we shall identify the exact point at which they have officially joined the profession.

This is the story of "Fred." Fred was never much of a joiner. He preferred to spend time with his laptop and BlackBerry rather than sitting in meetings. One organization, however, did catch his eye. He had always enjoyed playing chess, and he read in the newspaper about a new local unit of chess players being organized. He started attending and enjoyed the camaraderie and games that followed each meeting.

The first few meetings of the chess club went smoothly, carried by the fresh exuberance of something new and exciting. Then, problems began to develop. Differences of opinion emerged on how to set up a local tournament. The club needed more funds to send representatives to state and national tournaments. It needed better local publicity to attract more members. These and other issues sometimes became contentious, and the rancor of poorly run business meetings began to affect the morale of the fledgling organization.

The officers of the local club had no experience in running meetings, and it wasn't long before things started spiraling out of control. Everyone could see that order was required, but no one seemed to know how to bring order to the meetings. Following one of the more disorderly meetings, someone suggested that the club needed a parliamentarian to advise the officers. Fred had made no enemies up to this point, so he seemed a good choice. The officers approached Fred, and he agreed to serve as the club parliamentarian.

Fred picked up a copy of *Robert's Rules of Order Newly Revised*[1] at the local bookstore and started reading it, trying to figure out what he could do to help make the meetings of the chess club more orderly. After several failed attempts, he finally decided on a course of action. First, he would meet with the officers to help draft an agenda for each meeting. Then, he would ensure that the proposed agenda was adopted by a vote at the beginning of each meeting. Finally, he would meet with the president to ensure that this officer understood the importance of adhering to the adopted agenda and knew how to enforce an orderly consideration of all items on the agenda one at a time.

Fred's plan worked. Members quickly came to appreciate that their new parliamentarian had indeed found a plan for bringing order to their meetings. As time passed, the officers and members began to rely more and more on Fred's advice for keeping order. Business meetings were shorter and more efficient. Everyone could see that decisions were being made more quickly but with fairness to everyone.

Then, Fred began to change. As club members came to rely on him for keeping the meetings orderly, Fred began to see the business meetings in a different way. He had joined the club for a simple reason, to play chess and meet others who enjoyed the game. He had not paid much attention to the problems of running meetings until the membership drafted him to serve as club parliamentarian. Now, however, Fred was cast in the role of parliamentarian—the club's expert on meeting procedures.

In his new role, Fred began to pay attention to things that he had never noticed before. How long were members allowed to speak? Were they staying on the topic under discussion, or did they stray? How were votes taken? Were the votes always correctly counted, and did members understand the result of each vote? Fred began to pay less and less attention to the issues, and more and more attention to the procedures. He was now being transformed into a parliamentarian.

As Fred became more accustomed to his new role, he found that he actually liked it. Although he had never paid much attention to meeting procedures before joining the chess club, Fred now started reading books and articles about meeting procedures. The more he read, the easier his job became. Members appreciated Fred's newfound expertise, and word began to spread outside the club that Fred could bring order to any meeting.

Eventually, word of Fred's expertise reached a swimming club that held its meetings in the same building as the chess club. The swimming club was having problems with its meetings. The officers couldn't seem to control things, and eventually the members realized that help was needed. They decided to ask Fred if he would come and help bring order to their meetings. As luck would have it, Fred was afraid of water and couldn't swim a single stroke without fear of drowning.

Recognizing that the swimming club did not expect him to swim, Fred agreed to serve as temporary parliamentarian, at least until some order was restored. He started attending meetings and quickly gained the confidence of the members. They could see that Fred was bringing a new orderliness to their meetings. Fred was now widely accepted as a competent parliamentarian for both the chess club and the swimming club. Other organizations began to hear about Fred's newfound expertise. He was now gaining recognition as a parliamentarian.

Fred's story is not unusual. It illustrates how many people are unexpectedly called on to serve as a parliamentarian. Most of them have no special training. They simply join a club, get pressed into service, and then start reading whatever they can find about meeting procedures. The question to be considered here is whether these club members actually become members of the parliamentary profession, and if so, at what point do they make the transition to join the profession?

To answer the question, let's return to the story of Fred. At what point did Fred ally himself with the parliamentary profession? Was it when he joined the chess club? No, he was just a club member at that time. Was it when he agreed to serve as club parliamentarian for the chess club? No, he was still in his primary role as a club member, although he now performed a new function. Was it when he agreed to serve as parliamentarian for the swimming club? Yes, he was now officially a member of the parliamentary profession.

The question then arises as to why Fred's joining the swimming club was so different from his membership in the chess club. The difference is that Fred was a chess player, and he had a vested interest in the chess club. Any decisions that were made by the chess club directly affected Fred. Although he was drafted to serve as parliamentarian, he still had a direct interest in all the substantive issues to come before the chess club.

It was different with the swimming club. Fred couldn't swim and had no interest at all in the outcome of any issues to be discussed and voted on during meetings of the swimming club. His only interest in coming to meetings was to assist with procedures. Since Fred had no interest in the outcome of any votes taken by the swimming club, he was probably a better parliamentarian for the swimming club than for the chess club. During meetings of the swimming club, Fred, as an outsider, was able to focus exclusively on procedural issues.

Notice that it made no difference whether Fred was paid to attend meetings of the swimming club. As a novice parliamentarian, Fred probably donated his newfound skills to the clubs that invited him to their meetings. At a later stage, Fred would be given honorariums in recognition of his efforts. His ties to the profession would be completed when he joined a professional association, paid dues, and committed to uphold the standards of professional excellence set forth in the code of ethics for parliamentarians. Further down the road, Fred would begin charging fees and expenses to attend meetings. The escalation of fees, however, is irrelevant to Fred's professionalism. Fred established himself as a professional the minute he jumped from the chess club to the swimming club. The critical factor that made him a member of the parliamentary profession was that Fred, not being a swimmer, attended meetings as an outsider and, therefore, was able to focus exclusively on procedures.

> MEMBERS OF THE PARLIAMENTARY PROFESSION
> ARE THOSE WHO ATTEND MEETINGS FOR THE
> SOLE PURPOSE OF ADVISING ON
> MATTERS OF PROCEDURE.

Now that we have established Fred and many others like him as bona fide members of the parliamentary profession, we need to look at the nature of the profession itself. Unlike many other professions, practice as a parliamentarian does not require licensure. Once a profession acquires licensure, state regulatory agencies gain control over the profession and set minimum standards for entry, uniform testing requirements, acceptable standard practices, disciplinary procedures, and continuing education requirements. Without licensure, a member of a profession can claim to be many things, but the client must trust that the claims are true. Without licensure, a résumé is only as valid as the testimonials provided by current or past clients.

The National Association of Parliamentarians (NAP) and the American Institute of Parliamentarians (AIP) have attempted to fill the void created by the absence of licensure. They have established levels of recognized competence with testing and minimum required standards for each level. They have set up continuing education programs for their members. They have established referral services for qualified members who request this service. They have also collaborated in the adoption of a joint code of ethics prescribing minimum standards of conduct for members of the profession.

Today, approximately 600 members of the profession are credentialed through NAP, AIP, or both associations.[2] These members pay dues and operate under the protective umbrella of one or both associations. Many of them carry professional liability insurance marketed through the two associations. They attend and teach at conventions, seminars, and workshops which may be offered by either association, or in some cases, events that are jointly sponsored by both associations.

Some might argue that members of the profession are restricted to the credentialed members of NAP and AIP. This distinction, however, results in an extremely small fraction of those who practice as parliamentarians. It ignores the many who started as a club parliamentarian and later found satisfaction in working with other organizations to improve their meeting procedures. It ignores many college professors and teachers who taught parliamentary procedure for years and then decided to apply their knowledge as a practicing parliamentarian. It also ignores many self-taught individuals who have never joined an association of parliamentarians but who are highly competent and run their own business as professional parliamentarians.

In conclusion, then, it seems reasonable to define the members of the profession in terms of how they relate to their clients rather than on the basis of association membership or credentialing. Members of the profession, as defined and discussed in this book, are those who attend meetings for the sole purpose of advising on matters of procedure.

Chapter Two

The Parliamentarian of Today

The similarities among today's parliamentarians are obvious. They attend meetings for the sole purpose of advising on meeting procedures. They pay attention to detail. They insist that rules be followed and that order be maintained. These traits are, or should be, common to all parliamentarians. But what about the differences?

An important distinction may be made between those who are members of a parliamentary association and those who are not. As we have seen, NAP and AIP provide many services to their members, including regular scheduling of workshops and seminars, sale of educational materials, and credentialing and job placement programs.

Many parliamentarians, however, do not belong to either NAP or AIP, and in fact, many have not heard of either association. Club members like Fred are often isolated from the national associations. Members of this group are usually self-taught and have never been tested on their knowledge of parliamentary procedure. They have no opportunities to network with other members of the profession and do not receive publications. NAP and AIP are constantly trying to reach out to this group, but the obstacles to identification and communication with members of this group are formidable.

Another distinction may be seen in the practice of charging fees, which is usually correlated with experience. Those with the most experience will usually charge the highest fees, and those with little or no experience charge little or nothing. Those in the latter category are often working to gain experience and are more than happy to donate their expertise wherever it may be helpful. There are also many instances where highly experienced parliamentarians have donated their services pro bono. Work may be donated to organizations that need help but can ill afford to pay the standard rate charged by experienced professionals.

A further distinction should be made between those who practice as advisors and those who perform in other roles such as teachers, research assistants, and professional presiders. It is true that many parliamentarians have broadened their practice to include these and other functions. *Robert's Rules*, however, defines the central role of a parliamentarian as an advisor on procedural matters.[3] Procedures are "home base" for parliamentarians, and members of the profession, as defined in this book, are those who attend meetings for the sole purpose of advising on matters of procedure.

Another distinction among members of the profession is between those who view their profession as a business and those who regard it as a hobby, form of entertainment, or diversion. Unlike members of other professions who make a living practicing their profession, relatively few parliamentarians depend on their practice as their sole source of income. Many members of the profession, however, have built a highly successful business. These members keep scrupulous financial records and regularly report taxable income—minus business expenses—to the Internal Revenue Service. Business oriented members have their own printed stationery, business cards, and brochures advertising their business. They maintain Web sites and publish scholarly articles as members of the profession. The nonbusiness parliamentarian, on the other hand, takes a much more relaxed view of the profession and takes only occasional jobs that are convenient. Many members of this group do not charge fees simply because they do not want the responsibility of running a business and they do not want to spend a lot of time filling out forms.

Finally, there are vast differences among members of the profession in their educational backgrounds. Unlike other professions that require a degree for admission to the profession, the parliamentary profession has no minimum requirement for formal education. The profession has, however, attracted many highly educated members. Meetings of parliamentarians may include doctors, lawyers, college professors, communication consultants, nurses, and members of many other professions who have found a second career in parliamentary procedure.

Client organizations are often delighted to find that their parliamentary consultant brings much more experience and expertise to the job than just making a passing grade on a written examination. The sharp variation in the educational backgrounds of parliamentarians, however, sometimes makes it difficult to match the right parliamentarian to the needs of the client. Client organizations who hire several different parliamentarians over time are often amazed at the differences. They quickly learn that parliamentarians have little in common beyond their exclusive focus on meeting procedures.

> # THE ONE THING
> # THAT MEMBERS OF THE PROFESSION
> # SHARE IN COMMON IS THEIR FOCUS
> # ON MEETING PROCEDURES.

Like members of other professions, parliamentarians develop specialty areas and tend to focus their practice mostly within these specialties. A brief overview of the most common specialty areas includes the following:

1. Specialist in the application of *Robert's Rules*

This is probably the most common specialty, especially among those with limited experience. Many parliamentarians pride themselves on their in-depth knowledge of the latest edition. They may have memorized sections of the manual by rote. They may limit their practice to organizations that prescribe the use of *Robert's Rules* in their bylaws. This group of specialists commonly insists on using the exact terminology that is in the book, and they are very strict in matters of protocol.

2. Specialist in crisis management

Some parliamentarians tend to seek out organizations in which a crisis has been building and has been left unattended for months. This group thrives when an entire board of directors is so stressed that they are ready to resign as a block, when a motion is pending to remove the president from office, or when a lawsuit from a disgruntled member threatens to bankrupt the organization. Members of this group usually charge the highest fees and collect all or most of their money up front before any service has been rendered.

3. Specialist in legal documents

Some parliamentarians focus on the legal aspects of parliamentary law. They go beyond collecting state codes and certificates of incorporation and study court cases in which legal precedents have been set. They may often be found consulting with the organization's legal counsel. The legalistic approach to parliamentary procedure has solid historical precedent. The profession did, after all, originate in the English parliament. It came to this country through the application of English common law to legislative bodies, and later to voluntary societies in the United States. Many of the procedural manuals now in use were written by attorneys or law students.

4. Specialist in one type of organization

Many parliamentarians limit their practice exclusively to nonprofit associations, homeowners associations, church affiliated organizations, political organizations, labor unions, health related organizations, or other specialty types. The advantage of limiting one's practice to these organizational types is that each category develops its own unique vocabulary for doing business. Some specialty types, such as homeowners associations, require mastery of an entire body of complex legislation to adequately serve the client's needs. Specialization of this type makes the parliamentarian's job easier and is usually more satisfying to the client.

Despite the segmentation of the profession into various areas of specialty, there remains a core of common values and required competencies that bind the profession together. These are the building blocks that constitute the underpinnings of our profession. The following list is not all inclusive but is sufficiently representative to give an accurate picture of The Parliamentarian of Today:

1. Competence in the use of *Robert's Rules*

As discussed in Chapter Three, *Robert's Rules* is indeed the centerpiece of our profession. No parliamentarian should attempt to practice without a firm grasp on the use of the manual. Extensive memorizing of details is not necessary, but competence in using the book to locate answers quickly is essential. Even when the organization's bylaws prescribe the use of a different parliamentary authority, the parliamentarian recognizes Robert as home base.

2. Competence in the application of principles

Parliamentarians are committed to the principle of majority rule. The purpose of having meetings is to discover and implement the will of the majority. On the other hand, the right of the minority to a fair hearing must be protected. Parliamentarians understand the importance of these and other principles discussed in Chapter Five. They understand that rules must never violate basic principles.

3. Competence in education

Parliamentarians are not expected to be professional educators but they recognize that education is often the most important part of a job, as discussed in Chapter Six. Workshops for members are an essential part of the members' preparation to participate in business meetings. Parliamentarians are also called upon to do board training and sometimes to provide individual tutoring to key officers regarding their oral performance during meetings. Parliamentarians must also be prepared to explain complex motions when called upon during business meetings.

4.   Competence in oral communication

Oral skills come into play when communicating with the presiding officer, explaining motions to members, or teaching workshops. College level courses in public speaking, mediation, and related subjects are highly recommended. Parliamentarians quickly learn that they cannot use the unabridged language of *Robert's Rules* for all their clients. The ability to communicate at the *client's* level is critical. Chapter Seven describes tense situations in which mediation skills can also be very helpful.

5.   Competence in written communication

Writing skills are crucial for composing and revising motions, bylaws, standing rules, and special rules of order. Parliamentarians must also be proficient in writing scripts. Many parliamentarians write detailed scripts for every meeting and backup scripts to accommodate various scenarios that may develop during the meeting. A good script contains every word that is spoken from the dais, and good rehearsals can make a scripted meeting appear unscripted.

6.   Competence in ethics

The parliamentarian will, at all times, have an understanding and acceptance of the ethical standards of the profession, as set forth in Chapter Eight, and will adhere to those standards in both personal and professional conduct. The parliamentarian strives to avoid even the slightest appearance of ethical misconduct.

7.   Competence in the interpretation of governing documents

The parliamentarian is frequently called upon to help interpret and apply the provisions of a bylaw or standing rule. Although not an attorney, the parliamentarian is familiar with the organization's certificate of incorporation and the applicable state codes. The parliamentarian understands the legal parameters of the profession as set forth in Chapter Nine, develops a working relationship with the association's legal counsel, and defers to legal counsel for a legal opinion when appropriate.

The competencies discussed above shape the many tasks performed by members of the profession. The chapters that follow will discuss the building blocks of the profession, how each of these has contributed to the education and development of The Parliamentarian of Today, and how they are likely to transform The Parliamentarian of Tomorrow.

Building Blocks of the Parliamentary Profession

CHAPTER THREE

Robert:
The Centerpiece of Our Profession

Parliamentarians often describe themselves as experts in using *Robert's Rules*, referring to the latest edition of *Robert's Rules of Order Newly Revised*. The fact is that *Robert's Rules* has dominated the profession ever since its first printing in 1876, and its influence is unlikely to diminish for the foreseeable future. It is absolutely mandatory that any aspiring parliamentarian study this manual. Further, a theoretical knowledge of *Robert's Rules* will not be enough; the parliamentarian must also be an expert in the practical application of the rules. The parliamentarian's education must include hands-on workshops that focus on practical skills such as presiding; processing motions; and writing scripts, opinions, and bylaw amendments.

In addition to the latest edition of *Robert's Rules*, the parliamentarian's library should minimally include *Parliamentary Law*[4] and *Robert's Rules of Order Newly Revised in Brief.*[5] The former contains detailed explanations of the rules set forth in the parliamentary manual. The latter is a simplified guide to using *Robert's Rules* with many cross references to the manual. Curious parliamentarians may also wish to examine Robert's *Parliamentary Practice* published in 1921 as the first elementary text based on *Robert's Rules*.

The manner in which *Robert's Rules* became so quickly and widely accepted by voluntary societies in the United States is a remarkable story. Henry M. Robert was an engineering officer in the United States Army who eventually attained the rank of brigadier general. His interest in parliamentary procedure began when, while still a lieutenant, he was elected to chair a meeting in New Bedford, Massachusetts, in 1863. Lacking firm guidelines for serving as chairman, Robert left the meeting both embarrassed and determined to be better prepared for future meetings. The life of an officer on active duty was difficult, and Robert was compelled to devote most of his time moving to assigned locations around the country and overseeing construction. His study of meeting procedures was mostly restricted to the winter months when harsh weather prohibited much outside work.

Robert's first book of rules, published in 1876 as *Robert's Rules of Order*, was based on practices of the U.S. House of Representatives. Robert had studied the efforts of Luther S. Cushing (1803-1856) to adapt legislative rules to the needs of ordinary societies. Cushing, however, had confined his manual to matters of English common law and had recommended that each organization adopt its own rules of order. Most organizations had proved unable to improvise adequate supplementary rules for their own use; hence, Robert confronted a market in confusion. Robert was the first to attempt to standardize the parliamentary practices of ordinary societies, and his first edition sold out within a few months. He quickly gained a national reputation for his standardized procedures, and he received hundreds of letters raising questions that would be covered in subsequent expanded editions. A family tradition was born, and later editions have remained largely under the control of the original Robert family and its heirs to the present day.

Parliamentarians today have many resources through which to study specific applications of *Robert's Rules*. The Robert's Rules of Order Web site maintains a list of frequently asked questions, provides official interpretations by the authors of *Robert's Rules*, and sponsors a question-and-answer forum in which anyone can participate.[6] Both NAP[7] and AIP[8] offer a large collection of study and teaching materials based on *Robert's Rules*. Both organizations sell the current edition of *Robert's Rules* in hardback, paperback, or a CD version indexed for instant research by chapter, topic, or key word.

Darwin Patnode has aptly noted that "American parliamentary law after 1875 is largely the history of Henry M. Robert's influence and the revolt against it."[9] Indeed, *Robert's Rules* has been at the epicenter of almost everything written about parliamentary procedure for voluntary societies since the publication of his first edition. Rule books that have, in varying degrees, challenged Robert are discussed in Chapter Four.

Some members of the legal profession have mounted their own challenge to Robert based on court decisions and legal precedent. Howard L. Oleck cites numerous instances in which Robert "created" or "invented" his own rules, which have not been upheld by the courts.[10] Paul Mason, making a direct attack on Robert, states that "the courts will apply the rules of parliamentary law as laid down by judicial decisions and not according to General Robert . . . Many of the rules in parliamentary manuals, by Robert and other laymen, are not

parliamentary law, and . . . there is no assurance that an organization can follow them and have its actions upheld by a court of law."[11] Perhaps, in response to these attacks from members of the legal profession, it is significant that all nonfamily members of the *Robert's Rules* authorship team are attorneys.

Robert has, from the beginning, enjoyed strong support from the profession, and an important body of literature has emerged that lends credibility to his work. This group of authors does not challenge Robert but attempts to simplify, explain, and apply his rules. In 1940, J. Jeffery Auer produced his *Esssentials of Parliamentary Procedure* which was "compatible" with *Robert's Rules* and presented "only the *essentials* of parliamentary procedure." More recently, Lena Hardcastle's *Parliamentary Law Rules and Procedures for Conducting Conventions*[12] is a good example of a specialized application based on *Robert's Rules*. Darwin Patnode's Modern Edition of *Robert's Rules of Order*[13] tries to "retain the best of the original style and content of Robert's ideas" of the 1876 edition, "and supplement them with modern language and rules." Jon Ericson's *Notes and Comments on Robert's Rules* emphasizes "the simple machinery in *Robert*," and seeks to "encourage members to obtain and study, rather than shy away from, *Robert's Rules of Order Newly Revised*."[14]

It was once fashionable to attack *Robert's Rules*, particularly following publication of the first *Newly Revised* edition in 1970, which disappointed many who had expected major changes in language and perhaps some simplification of the rules. The attacks have largely subsided, and *Robert's Rules* is now almost universally held to be the supreme authority of the profession. The next chapter will explore how parliamentarians have, in their own practice, dealt with the other authorities who, in varying degrees, have attempted to replace *Robert's Rules* with other rules.

In summary, General Henry M. Robert was a true genius of his time, working with only minimal guidelines and breaking new ground in the development of rules suitable for ordinary nonlegislative assemblies. His influence on the profession has not diminished and is likely to continue for the foreseeable future. The dominance of his rules dictates that all parliamentarians, even those who serve organizations that have rejected *Robert's Rules* in favor of a different authority, must be conversant with *Robert's Rules*.

> IT IS ABSOLUTELY MANDATORY
> THAT ANY ASPIRING PARLIAMENTARIAN
> STUDY THIS MANUAL.

Chapter Four

Building Block: Other Authorities

It may seem disrespectful to lump together all the other authors who have written manuals of parliamentary procedure. However, if one were to visualize the size of the building blocks that have shaped our profession, the size of Robert's block would exceed that of all the others combined. This does not mean that all except Robert should be ignored. A strong argument can be made that everyone who aspires to be a professional in the field should have significant exposure to at least one authority besides Robert.

Who are these writers, and what are they trying to prove? First, they implicitly recognize the supremacy of Robert. Some attack his work, others simply try to build on it. In one way or another they use Robert's ideas as a beginning point for their own rule book. Second, they all try to make rules more easily comprehended and useable for the average citizen who has little or no background in parliamentary procedure. Third, unlike Robert whose manual is comprehensive in scope, these writers tend to focus on procedures most likely to be used on a regular basis. They admit that their works do not necessarily encompass all the procedural needs that may arise. Rather than clutter their books with detail, they leave it to the organization to handle the occasional glitch that organizations encounter from time to time. Fourth, all these writers emphasize the primacy of principles over rules, a concept that will be developed further in the next chapter.

The writers who make up the list of other authors are legion, and it is impossible to recognize all of them here. My selection of Sturgis, Demeter, Hellman, Keesey, Farwell, Cannon, and Lochrie are arbitrary choices. These authors, however, provide an excellent sampling of the many worthwhile contributions to our profession in addition to those of the *Robert's Rules* authorship team.

Alice F. Sturgis's *Standard Code of Parliamentary Procedure,* based on over 3,000 cases involving legal questions dealing with parliamentary procedure,[15] developed into the first major challenge to *Robert's Rules.* Although not attacking Robert by name, Sturgis's criteria for selecting a parliamentary authority clearly have Robert in their sights:

A parliamentary authority should be so clear and simple that anyone can understand it . . . .

It should be so complete that no other book or research will be needed. It should omit needless or outmoded procedures . . . It must present parliamentary law so accurately that the courts will uphold any action taken according to the rules it states.[16]

The first two editions are filled with legal citations of court cases, and Sturgis repeatedly makes the case that her rules are more closely allied with court decisions than *Robert's Rules.* The third and fourth editions, authored by a committee of AIP after Sturgis's death, dropped the court citations but continued the tradition of simplifying and streamlining the rules. The *Standard Code,* adopted by the medical profession and some other groups, remains one of the most influential manuals of rules next to Robert.

George Demeter's *Manual of Parliamentary Law and Procedure,* first published in 1948, was republished in 1969 as the famous Blue Book Edition.[17] Billed as a manual for the legal conduct of business in deliberative assemblies, the manual continued Sturgis's practice of including court citations for ready reference. Demeter described his book as easy to comprehend and apply at meetings and conventions and one that should be in every club member's home. Demeter's manual ranks second to Sturgis in being adopted by local organizations. Although Sturgis's and Demeter's manuals have been adopted by less than ten percent of all local societies, they have cultivated a loyal following and continue to exert a positive influence on the profession.

Hugo Hellman's book *Parliamentary Procedure,* published in 1966,[18] explicitly acknowledges the profession's indebtedness to Robert, but charges that "Robert's book is not a book from which the procedure can easily be learned."[19] Hellman states that his book, unlike that of Robert, is a textbook. The advantage of learning from a text is that "we need to learn only those rules which normally come into use in the affairs of the typical contemporary organizations to which you may expect to belong."[20] This 113-page text is one of the simplest manuals published in the field.

In 1971, shortly after publication of the first Newly Revised edition of *Robert's Rules,* Ray Keesey's *Modern Parliamentary Procedure* arrived on the scene.[21] Acknowledging that "progress in simplifying parliamentary rules has already been made by Hellman, Sturgis, and other recognized authorities," Keesey insists that "a need exists for greater simplification . . . despite previous efforts in this direction."[22] A unique feature of Keesey's book is the inclusion of a lengthy list of motions not recommended. Some, he claims, are too complicated. Others are "so infrequently used that they have never been heard in thousands of organizations." Still others are not necessary because "simpler and clearer methods for accomplishing the same purposes exist."[23]

In 1980, Hermon W. Farwell published his first edition of *The Majority Rules*.[24] Dedicated to the memory of Alice F. Sturgis, Farwell's 112-page book seeks even greater simplicity than its predecessors. Referring obliquely to a popular authority in which eighty-three motions and requests are needed, Farwell states that his manual considers sixteen completely adequate.[25] He also notes that less complex procedures promote active participation by members.

Continuing the tradition of simplification and practicality, Hugh Cannon published his first edition of *Cannon's Concise Guide to Rules of Order* in 1992.[26] A Rhodes scholar and graduate of Harvard Law School, Cannon served with distinction as parliamentarian for the Democratic National Committee and the National Education Association. His book focuses on twelve basic motions (compared to eighty-four in *Robert's Rules*) that cover the matters most likely to come before meetings.[27] He argues that rules should be simple and used as little as possible.[28] He also introduces the concept that complex procedures can be avoided by the chair's earning the goodwill of the assembly.

James Lochrie's *Meeting Procedures*, published in 2003, is designed to keep the rules simple.[29] The author presents his book as "a modern text on meeting procedure, taking into consideration new communication technologies and, more importantly, the modern business practices of organizations." Further, the book "avoids jargon by building on the advances of late twentieth-century English language usage in parliamentary law." Lochrie notes that "there is one constant in all the challenges and politics that occur within not-for-profit organizations—that decisions must be made that advance the aims of the organization," and most of these decisions are made at meetings.[30]

As we have seen, the authorities discussed above each have a somewhat different focus, but all of them are united in their emphasis on simplification and practicality. None of them claims to present a system of rules as comprehensive as Robert. Some of them claim to be in greater conformity with legal interpretations as cited in court cases. All of them build on underlying principles of the profession.

The above discussion of the other authorities leads us to a consideration of a major problem in the parliamentary profession. Some parliamentarians have unfortunately concluded that they need to study only the works of Henry

Robert. Some have gone so far as to say that they refuse to look at the works of any other author as this will only confuse them. These parliamentarians, I believe, are making a huge mistake and do a disservice to themselves, to their clients, and to the profession.

First, the credentials of the authors should be considered. As a group, they are highly educated members of the profession. Some are attorneys, some are university professors, all have practiced as professional parliamentarians. As a group, they have given much time to research and reflection. They represent some of the best talent of the profession. To simply ignore them is a waste.

More importantly, the parliamentarian who studies only a single authority will never gain the perspective required for professional work. This person tends to view every point in the book as equally important with every other point. A minor variation in language appears equally important as a matter of basic principle. A rule protecting the rights of the minority appears equally important as a minor requirement of protocol. The overall perspective becomes distorted, and something becomes important only because Robert said so rather than because of the intrinsic worth of the statement.

I have, on several occasions, observed parliamentarians on the dais whose education ended with *Robert's Rules*. They are almost always correct on what Robert says, but they are so focused on the book that they lose sight of the organization's needs. The presiding officer may need more guidance on the use of correct parliamentary terminology. Key issues may need to be rephrased in language that the members can understand. The parliamentarian who is too focused on *Robert's Rules* may miss opportunities to enhance communication between the presiding officer and the membership.

An analogy may be helpful to illustrate the futility of attempting professional practice from the perspective of having studied only Robert or any single authority. In my college teaching career of more than thirty years, I taught thousands of classes in public speaking. Beginning speakers often had problems in preparing their speeches, and part of my job was to give them the proper tools for advance preparation. They were learning to speak extemporaneously, which meant that they could not write out or memorize the speech. The pattern of ideas could be prepared in advance, but the words had to be chosen at the moment of utterance.

Some speakers would prepare by finding a single article in a magazine and basing their entire speech on that article. I advised against this practice of giving a single source speech. The student who gave such a speech would invariably end up memorizing parts of the article and repeating some of the author's language. It was, in effect, a partly memorized speech. The speech did not sound like the speaker's normal manner of speaking; it sounded like the person who wrote the article. As a teacher of public speaking, I could easily spot a single source speech, and such a speech was graded down for improper preparation.

Speakers who followed my instructions would read three or four articles on the same topic. By so doing, they gained a perspective on the topic that would be impossible to gain from reading a single article. After going through the process of selecting material from several different writers, the student now "owned" the speech. Having examined the topic from several points of view before composing the speech, the student attained a high level of comfort and exuded confidence while speaking.

I believe this analogy applies to members of our profession who prepare from only once source. Even if that source happens to be Robert, the centerpiece of our profession, the authorship team of *Robert's Rules* still comprises a single source. The parliamentarian who prepares entirely from one source will be seriously handicapped when real-life problems must be resolved in the course of professional practice.

This point is well understood by the profession's other authors. Keesey states that "special situations do arise that call for procedures not covered specifically in any manual."[31] Lochrie agrees, stating that "in some cases no rule may exist to cover a specific situation."[32] Cannon notes that the "rules of parliamentary procedure evolved over centuries and continue to change even now."[33]

The professional parliamentarian prepares by studying multiple sources and focusing on basic principles as well as specific rules. It is in the study of principles from multiple sources that the professional parliamentarian gains the perspective and flexibility required to deal with real-life situations that are routinely encountered in practice. The next building block of our profession, then, is the study of principles.

> THE PARLIAMENTARIAN
> WHO PREPARES FROM ONE SOURCE
> WILL BE SERIOUSLY HANDICAPPED.

CHAPTER FIVE

Building Block: Underlying Principles

From its earliest beginnings, a key building block of the parliamentary profession has been the study and application of basic principles. Principles may be defined as "the laws or facts of nature underlying the working of an artificial device."[34] If rules are conceived as man-made artificial devices for running meetings, then principles are regarded as more permanent, residing in nature, and providing a solid foundation for the rules.

If principles reside in nature and are permanent, one might expect that the authors of American rule books would agree on the underlying principles. Such, however, is not the case. Almost every author has their own list of principles different from every other author. Some of the authors have committed to one set of principles and then added to the list a few years later.

Robert, when preparing to write his *Pocket Manual of Rules of Order for Deliberative Assemblies*, settled on four basic principles as the foundation of his work, namely that (a) the majority must rule, (b) the minority must be heard, (c) the rights of individuals must be guarded, and

(d) justice and courtesy must prevail. He deemed these principles to be consistent with his "guiding star," which was to discover and implement "the will of the assembly.[35]

Later editions of *Robert's Rules* redefine the basic principles as protecting the rights of (a) the majority, (b) the minority, (c) individual members, and (d) absentees. This list, however, is not comprehensive, as new principles are scattered throughout *Robert's Rules*. Some examples are:

> The requirements for changing a previous action are greater than those for taking the action in the first place.[36]

Only one question can be considered at a time.[37]

One session cannot tie the hands of a majority at any later session.[38]

The authors who follow Robert, and who often attack his rules, are in substantial disagreement about which principles are considered "basic." Sturgis's first edition lists eleven principles: (a) facilitating the transaction of business, (b) the majority decides, (c) equal rights and privileges of all members, (d) protection of minority rights, (e) full and free discussion, (f) following the simplest and most direct procedure, (g) precedence of motions, (h) the member's right to information, (i) consideration of one question at a time, (j) choosing leaders through democratic process, and (k) impartiality of the presiding officer.[39] Sturgis's second edition eliminates items (f), (g), (i), (j), and (k) from the list and adds a new principle: fairness and good faith at meetings.[40]

The authors following Sturgis are split regarding the number of basic principles. Demeter lists five.[41]

Hellman and Keesey agree on four.[42] Farwell and Lochrie agree on six.[43] The four principles most commonly listed are (a) the right of the majority to rule, (b) the right of the minority to a fair hearing, (c) the equality of members, and (d) freedom of speech. We shall examine each of these in detail plus a new principle, added by Lochrie, regarding the efficiency of meetings.

The first and most important principle mentioned by almost all parliamentary authorities is the principle of majority rule. At first glance, this may seem absurdly simple. In our democratic culture in America, we have long been accustomed to democratic decision making in which the majority prevails. History, however, teaches us that this principle has been applied quite differently in other periods of history and other cultures. John Heinberg, in his "History of the Majority Principle," notes that in the 13th and 14th centuries, a majority was variously interpreted as a unanimous vote, or two-thirds, or four-sevenths. Even after the definition of majority became stable, the question persisted, "A majority of what?" Majority was made to depend upon both the quality and the quantity of votes.[44] The concept of specialization teaches that not all voters are equally informed or capable of voting intelligently. Darwin Patnode has recommended that the concept of specialization be considered by parliamentarians, and he suggests that the principle of majority rule, which many believe to be permanent and unchanging, could be modified in the future.[45]

In today's society, of course, the principle of majority rule is used for most decision making, however decision by consensus or a unanimous vote may be used whenever it is clear that no one objects to a proposed course of action. Once decided, the entire membership is expected to support the decision, at least until some future time that the decision might be rescinded. Exceptions to the principle of majority require a two-thirds vote for the amendment of bylaws, motions to close or limit debate, and other motions designed to protect minority rights. The exceptions, however, only reinforce the rule that most matters are decided by majority vote.

The second principle, closely allied to the principle of majority rule, is the protection of minority rights. The essential right of a minority is the right to a fair hearing. The minority, in effect, has the right to present its case in the hope that the hearers will change their position on the issue at hand. If enough members change, then the former majority becomes a minority, and the former minority becomes the majority. In parliamentary procedure, majorities and minorities are fleeting. During the course of a business meeting, a member may have voted with several majorities and several minorities and may have switched back and forth several times during the debate. In summary, every minority has the right to a fair hearing, with the hope that, in the course of debate, the minority will become the majority. The right to a fair hearing, however, does not extend indefinitely. After all sides have been heard, a vote should be taken. Voluntary societies do not allow filibusters which violate other basic principles.

A third principle widely recognized and applied in today's society is the equality of members. The chairman of a meeting is expected to treat all members fairly and not to give any one member an advantage over others during the meeting. Each member has exactly the same right to make motions, to debate, to vote, to run for office, and to serve on committees. If members perceive that some are being treated "more equally" than others, meetings are likely to become bitter and divisive. The best insurance to ensure fair treatment of all members is to provide whatever special training is needed for the chairman. The chairman is ultimately responsible to ensure that members receive equal and fair treatment.

The fourth principle agreed on by most parliamentarians is the requirement of full and free discussion of issues before taking a vote. This principle implies that members may not be intimidated and prevented from speaking their minds, nor can there be any form of punishment meted out to those who have opposed popular issues. This principle also implies that some meetings may become tense precisely because members are encouraged to say what they think. The opposite of full and free discussion is the railroading of certain issues and the suppression of dissent. Such tactics may result in a meeting that appears to run smoothly, but resentment and hostility are bound to surface when members feel that they have been mistreated.

Finally, the principle of efficiency, mentioned by Lochrie, appears important in today's society. As we have become a busier society than in times past, this principle may gain future momentum. Many families now have two wage earners, and therefore have less time to attend meetings. Our entire society has become clock oriented, moving rapidly from one task to another. This brings into question, then, the expectations of members who attend meetings. They want the security of knowing that a meeting scheduled for 7:30 p.m. to 9:00 p.m. will actually complete all its important business by 9:00 p.m. Parliamentary procedure has a number of built-in safeguards to help maintain efficiency, such as a call for the orders of the day, which insists upon following the adopted agenda. Lochrie notes that efficiency must be balanced by the concept of effectiveness, defined as "the ability to reach useful and well thought out decisions."[46]

Some of the earlier writers in the field may have felt that the basic principles of parliamentary procedure are permanent and unchanging. Alice Sturgis expressed the views of many educators in her statement that "if you learn the basic principles, it will be very easy to learn the rules because most of them follow logically from the principles."[47] It is true that principles underlie rules, and principles are the building blocks of rules. However, the priorities assigned to principles can and do change over time. In a slower paced society, it might have been advisable to allow a feisty minority two or three hours to present its arguments. In today's society, the principle of efficiency might very well mandate that a final decision be reached within an hour or less. As organizations act to update their rules and make them more responsive to the needs of members, parliamentarians need to be cognizant of the underlying principles in play.

Lochrie argues persuasively that principles that once seemed fundamental are sometimes abrogated or subordinated to another principle when a new rule is formulated. Principles come into conflict when a new rule must be formulated that both protects the right of the majority to rule and the right of the minority to oppose. The key to balancing these conflicting rights, he says, is for each organization to set their own rules for reasonableness. What is reasonable for one organization may be entirely unreasonable for another.[48]

Parliamentarians of the future may need to spend considerable time in researching the principles that underlie an organization's rules.[49] When demands for change occur, the parliamentarian must be ready to help identify the underlying principles and move the discussion forward. This level of service requires far more than simply reciting rules from a rule book.

Parliamentarians do indeed render distinctly different levels of service for their clients, and the services at each level are a direct result of the parliamentarian's education and training.

The first level of service is based on *Robert's Rules*. At this level, the parliamentarian simply quotes the rule from the book and stops. Parliamentarians entering the profession with only a basic knowledge of *Robert's Rules* probably cannot render service above this level.

At the second level, the parliamentarian looks for creative ways to apply the rules and gets directly involved in problem solving and crisis management. A parliamentarian with significant exposure to parliamentary authorities other than Robert can probably perform well at this level.

To get to the third level of service, the parliamentarian needs a thorough grounding in underlying principles and may also need specialized training in related areas such as communication, education, and technology. At this level, parliamentarians can provide service in crisis *prevention* (not just crisis management) and may also be helpful in clarifying an organization's mission, strategic goals, and priorities.

> TO GET TO THE HIGHEST LEVEL OF SERVICE,
> THE PARLIAMENTARIAN NEEDS
> A THOROUGH GROUNDING
> IN UNDERLYING PRINCIPLES.

CHAPTER SIX

Building Block: Educational Parameters

The parliamentary profession has a long history of alignment with the field of education. Many of the most prominent figures in the development of the parliamentary profession came from families aligned with education or were professional educators themselves. A few of the more prominent names are Alice Sturgis (professor, Stanford University), Robert W. English (teacher), Hugo Hellman (dean, School of Speech, Marquette University), J. Jeffery Auer (professor, Indiana University), Emil Pfister (professor, Central Michigan University), Greg Phifer (professor, Florida State University), Darwin Patnode (professor, University of Minnesota), and Rollie Cox (University of Wisconsin). Parliamentarians will also recall that Joseph Robert, father of Henry M. Robert, was a university president (Burlington University, Iowa).

The profession is well connected to the public schools and universities. Parliamentary procedure is often included in the curriculums although it is usually elective rather than required. I have personally seen parliamentary procedure taught at St. Louis University, Marquette University, and the State University of New York, College at Cortland. I have also taught parliamentary procedure to eighth grade students in the public schools with considerable success. Other educators with whom I have spoken have had similar experiences.

Parliamentary procedure has links to many disciplines and may be taught in conjunction with English, political science, communication studies, and other disciplines. Parliamentarians sometimes wonder aloud where the home of the profession may be found in the universities. The contemporary answer is in departments of communication studies. The logic of this location is inescapable since parliamentary procedure provides a means for members of an organization to communicate with each other. Parliamentary procedure is, in fact, a form of organizational communication, one of the major areas of study within communication departments.

In some respects, the parliamentary profession has not yet found its home in academia. This is because no degree program is offered for parliamentarians. Departments of communication studies offer isolated courses in parliamentary procedure, but no degree program. Parliamentarians hope for the day when parliamentary procedure will move out of the communication departments and will be organized as separate departments of parliamentary procedure offering degree programs in the discipline.

A strong thrust toward education is at the very core of the parliamentary profession. Within the two national associations, educational events are prolific. NAP has many local units that offer educational programs on a regular basis to their members as well as to the general public. AIP chapters perform much the same function, constantly educating and updating their members on the latest developments in the profession.

NAP and AIP also offer workshops, seminars, and practicums throughout the United States. Both offer correspondence courses to supplement the on-site offerings, and both have continuing education requirements for their credentialed members.

Beginning parliamentarians are often unprepared for the enormous scope of the education programs offered by NAP and AIP. Mock meetings and presiding exercises are the most common forms of classroom activity. Presiding skills are deemed essential for the parliamentarian's training, and students are provided many opportunities to master the basics of presiding through trial and error.

Another link between the parliamentary profession and education may be found in the competitions sponsored by such groups as 4-H and FFA (Future Farmers of America). Parliamentarians are constantly asked to volunteer their time either to coach teams preparing for competition or to serve as judges for competing teams. NAP and AIP encourage their members to participate in these events.

Education also plays an important role in the parliamentarian's relationship with client organizations. Beginning parliamentarians are often surprised to discover the many different roles in which they are expected to be proficient. In addition to teaching workshops, they may be required to meet with committees such as bylaws, tellers, and rules for the purpose of providing basic instructions to committee members. If the chairman is inexperienced, the parliamentarian may provide tutoring and/or coaching as needed. When complex motions threaten to hamper the work of the association, the parliamentarian may be called upon to explain (i.e., teach) the rules in such a way that they can be easily understood. The opportunities for teaching client organizations are almost infinite.

Most parliamentarians are not professional educators and have little or no training in how to teach. Most of their training as parliamentarians is tilted toward learning the rules, presiding, and advising clients. The American Institute of Parliamentarians is presently attempting to fill the gap by offering a teacher training course. Members who are credentialed by either AIP or NAP may take the course for the purpose of acquiring basic teaching skills. Parliamentarians entering the profession quickly learn that they must become teachers as well as advisors on meeting procedures. The expectation to teach as well as to advise is always present and should be anticipated as part of the parliamentarian's job description. A lack of formal training in education does not relieve the parliamentarian of a fundamental responsibility to teach. This need must be anticipated and should be an important part of a parliamentarian's training to enter the profession. It is not appropriate for the parliamentarian to ask, "Do I have to teach?" A better question is, "How can a parliamentarian *not* teach?" It's part of the job description!

The preparation of the parliamentarian to teach progresses naturally through three stages. First, the parliamentarian must master the rules and principles of parliamentary procedure, preferably through the eyes of more than one parliamentary authority. Second, the parliamentarian must have highly refined skills in writing, reading, and oral communication. Third, the parliamentarian needs to acquire basic teaching skills.

The above three areas of preparation have usually been deemed sufficient for parliamentarians as they prepare to teach and serve their clients, but a fourth skill has now appeared on the horizon. Parliamentarians of the future will be expected to know the technology of electronic meetings. They will also be expected to teach the correct uses of technology to their clients.

The bookstores of NAP and AIP are filled with materials to help the parliamentarian teach effectively. Flash cards, scripted mock meetings, charts and tables, and many other teaching aids can be helpful. It is also recommended that every parliamentarian enroll for at least one hands-on course to increase teaching effectiveness.

Will the need for trained teachers increase or decrease in the future? I think there is little doubt that the need for teaching skills will increase, especially in the area of technological change discussed in Chapter Ten.

> HOW CAN A PARLIAMENTARIAN *NOT* TEACH?
> IT'S PART OF THE JOB DESCRIPTION!

CHAPTER SEVEN

Building Block:
Communication Parameters

To Fred, it seemed like much more than four years ago that he had joined the local chess club. So much had happened since then. Now he was in demand by many organizations, and not all of them were local. His business had expanded to include three nonprofit state organizations and two national organizations. Now he would have a chance to serve an international organization meeting at a major convention center with 1,500 elected delegates in attendance.

Being a parliamentarian had become Fred's passion. For the past four years he had been preparing himself in many different ways for his first international convention. The credentialing examinations that he passed three years ago now seemed like a distant memory. After passing his exams, he had started attending NAP and AIP gatherings where he soon found himself in demand as a workshop presenter.

Fred had never been much of a public speaker, so he decided to take a course in public speaking at a local community college. To his surprise, he actually enjoyed the course. Before long, his workshops began to "sizzle" with his newfound public speaking skills. He appeared confident and relaxed. He was able to use light humor in a way that he never had before. Most importantly, he was able to reach his audience at *their* level, a critical skill when teaching parliamentary procedure to a group that barely understood how to make a main motion. He was becoming more and more convinced that his oral communication skills were essential for his work as a parliamentarian.

Fred's interest in oral communication quickly spread to other areas, including interpersonal communication, organizational communication, and mediation. He enrolled for a course in mediation. This course seemed a good fit for him because he already had some of the required skills. Neutrality, objectivity, and confidentiality were already built into his client relationships. As a parliamentarian, he had experience in playing the role of a neutral third party for resolving disputes. All he had to do now was to hone his skills in problem solving. Fred began to see that parliamentary procedure and mediation actually worked together to help members resolve their differences and get through their important business.

With the convention just three months away, Fred secured his signed contract with his newest client organization. He had learned through experience to be cautious and thorough when drafting the contract. One of Fred's early clients had tried to seat him in the front row facing the dais, a position from which it was impossible to give advice to the presiding officer. Fred had learned his lesson, and now he inserted a clause into every contract to ensure that he would be seated next to the chairman during business meetings. Another of Fred's earlier organizations had put Fred into a double occupancy hotel room with a member of the board of directors. That arrangement had not worked out too well. The two roommates were constantly moving on different time schedules, and neither got much rest. Fred's contracts now guaranteed him a private room. Fred had also discovered that he could do a more thorough job of preparation if he arrived at the convention site several days early, so this provision was incorporated into Fred's contracts.

With the contract signed and only three months to go, Fred developed a list of all the things he had to do before traveling to the convention site. He knew that thorough preparation was the most important part of his job, and he had made certain, in drafting the terms of the contract, that he would be well compensated for his preparation time. His "to do" list was extensive and included the following:

1. Get copies of all governing documents, the meeting agenda, proposed bylaw amendments, recent minutes, and proposed convention rules.
2. Arrange a private consultation at the convention site with the presiding officer.
3. Get lists of names of officers, board members, and key committee chairs.
4. Ensure that the lines of communication are open to the presiding officer and the executive office and encourage any procedural questions to come to the parliamentarian as early as possible.
5. Arrange for parliamentary workshop(s) for the members, and perhaps for the board of directors.

6. Do advance preparation for the workshops, including preparation of teaching aids and media presentations.
7. Study all relevant documents.
8. Arrange for an on-site script review session.
9. Work with staff to prepare the script.
10. Prepare backup scripts for procedural contingencies.
11. Find out which committees will need the parliamentarian to attend meetings.
12. Find out when key committees will be meeting and plan attendance accordingly.
13. Set up parliamentarian hours when delegates can consult during the convention and ensure that these hours are published and announced to the delegates.
14. Find out which issues may become contentious during the convention.
15. Find out as much as possible about competing factions and what strategies they are likely to employ.

Fred's first step toward implementation, then, was to call the executive director (who had signed his contract), order copies of all the documents he needed, ask some pertinent questions about the membership and the issues to come before the delegates, and ensure that the staff knew how to reach him with any questions or problems that might arise. He contacted the staff who would be writing the script and established deadlines for each phase of script development. He contacted the president to arrange a time and place for a conference and reviewed key issues and motions likely to come before the delegates.

While waiting for documents to arrive, Fred began preparing two workshops, one for the board of directors and one for first-time delegates. Using the communication skills gained at his local community college, Fred was careful to adapt each workshop to the level of the audience. He recognized that his language and style of teaching would have to be very different for an experienced board of directors compared to that required for a group of first-time delegates.

Fred's most important preparation, however, was in dealing with issues, especially one hot button issue that threatened to erupt on the convention floor. The board of directors had acted aggressively during the year, and most members of the board were proud of the board's accomplishments. Several powerful factions, however, felt very strongly that the board had exceeded its authority. Rumors circulated about resolutions of censure and possible measures to remove board members from office. Fred was dismayed when he received a letter from the president, submitted on behalf of the board, asking what would be the consequences if the entire board resigned prior to the opening of the convention.

Upon arrival at the convention site, Fred could see the gathering of cliques and factions in the hallways. He was summoned to the president's suite where the president, the executive director, and the vice president were waiting for him. A series of informal meetings with key factions was planned prior to the official opening of the convention, and they wanted Fred to attend. Anxious to be kept in the loop, Fred quickly agreed.

For several days, Fred spent most of his time in informal meetings. Leaders of the key factions were encouraged to meet face-to-face with board members. Differences of opinion were discussed openly. Following the initial hostilities, attempts were made to find areas of agreement and/or compromise. Fred's skills in mediation were tested at these meetings.

The meetings leading up to the official convention were intense, and Fred was deeply involved at every level. As the meetings continued, it became evident that some of the key factions were willing to modify their positions. Some board members became more sensitive to what the delegates were saying. Fred sensed an opening, and he began to use his mediation skills more aggressively.

By the time of the opening of the convention nearly a full week of intense communication had occurred. There had been no motions and no parliamentary procedure. Fred's only use of procedures had occurred in the script review session, where various contingencies were explored and backup scripts were developed in case certain floor fights were to erupt.

The convention itself progressed smoothly up to the point where the controversial agenda item would be introduced. When the president announced the next item on the agenda, Fred was ready with his script in front of him, his book of rules open to the right page, a copy of the agenda, a stack of governing documents, and a notepad. Then a member rose and made a motion. It was precisely the motion that Fred had been dealing with all week, and it represented a compromise that the influential factions had struck with the board. The motion was seconded, and the chair asked for discussion. There was none. The vote was taken, and the motion was adopted unanimously. Fred knew instantly that his work was done. The purpose of the meeting had been accomplished, and members would go home satisfied.

ONE MOTION
WAS ADOPTED UNANIMOUSLY.
FRED'S WORK WAS DONE.

Looking back at what had occurred, Fred reflected on how he had prepared for that meeting. First, he had studied many complex procedures and had been thoroughly tested on the details of parliamentary procedure. After gaining some experience as a club parliamentarian, Fred had moved on to acquire communication skills. Once the contract was signed, Fred became engaged in writing scripts and preparing workshops.

Fred had also immersed himself in the issues confronting the delegates. Instead of standing aloof from the delegates, he had placed himself strategically at the center of the action. From this position, he acted essentially as a communications consultant. He had been hired as a parliamentarian, but only one main motion was moved and adopted unanimously. As a parliamentarian, he had very little to do. As a communications consultant, he had done a lot. His client was satisfied and was content to pay several thousand dollars to Fred for the service.

> COMMUNICATION
> AND PARLIAMENTARY PROCEDURE
> COMPLEMENT EACH OTHER
> AND WORK TOGETHER.

Had Fred done his job properly? At first glance, it may appear that he had done very little as a parliamentarian. From the client's point of view, however, Fred had given the organization exactly what it needed. He had enabled members to open the lines of communication and confront their issues directly. Whether this occurred during the informal meetings leading up to the convention or during the convention itself mattered little. What did matter was the end result. The members found themselves in unanimous support of a single resolution. Issues had been confronted. Compromises had been worked out. Areas of agreement had been identified, and members left the meeting feeling that they had accomplished something worthwhile. Board members and officers were happy too. They would remember Fred's contributions and would likely want to hire him again.

It is significant that the organization hired Fred not just for the services rendered, which were those mostly related to communication. Fred was also hired because of his expertise in parliamentary procedure. Everyone recognized that if the hostilities continued, Fred could find his way through a labyrinth of motions and distractions. Fred was hired, not just for services rendered, but for his availability to deal with complex meeting procedures. Leading up to the meeting, Fred had anticipated as many different scenarios as possible and had actually prepared a backup script for each contingency. In the event that the meeting had wandered away from any of those scenarios, Fred would have had to advise the chair directly without the benefit of a script. Some people feel that this is the real reason why parliamentarians are hired—to be available in case the meeting goes off script.

Client organizations, in effect, don't purchase a bundle of services; they purchase the parliamentarian's best effort to ensure that they will get their important business done fairly and efficiently. This level of service does not come cheaply; the parliamentarian who provides it must be constantly preparing for every conceivable distraction and deviation from the script. The parliamentarian who is hired primarily as a consultant on procedural matters often ends up working as a communications consultant as well.

> PARLIAMENTARIANS ARE HIRED
> FOR THE TIME WHEN THE MEETING
> GOES OFF SCRIPT.

CHAPTER EIGHT

Building Block: Ethical Parameters

A profession needs more than a definition and description of what its members do; it needs a statement of what the profession stands for. One can look for this in various locations such as a mission statement, the first two articles of the bylaws, or in some cases, a motto or slogan that has been adopted. The clearest reflection of an organization's values, however, is likely found in its code of ethics. Most codes of ethics are developed to clarify the organization's values to the general public as well as to its membership. Many codes also attempt to regulate the conduct of members.

Codes of ethics may be aspirational, educational, disciplinary, or any combination of these. Aspirational codes, which are usually short, state the ideals toward which members of the profession aspire. Educational codes attempt to educate the membership regarding conduct that is deemed acceptable or unacceptable. Educational codes may be quite lengthy, citing examples and case studies. A third type of code is disciplinary. This type of code, in addition to providing standards of conduct for the members, also provides a means of enforcement.

The means of enforcing disciplinary codes can be quite complex. A separate document may be required to specify which categories of behavior are subject to discipline, who is responsible for administering discipline, and the various options for administering discipline. The primary enforcement agency is usually an ethics committee whose composition, method of election, and term of office must be included in the bylaws. Another element of enforcement is an appeals procedure, which permits members who have been disciplined by the ethics committee to appeal to a higher authority, such as the association's board of directors.

It is important to distinguish between the ethical framework of an association and the law. One who breaks the law may be prosecuted regardless of any code of ethics. Similarly, a member who has not broken any law can be punished for violating a code. Serious offenses may face both legal prosecution and disciplinary action by the profession.

The maximum penalty that can be administered for violating a code of ethics is revocation of membership in a professional association. Less serious violations can result in fines, temporary suspension of membership, or other remedies. Recognizing the possibility of retaliatory lawsuits, ethics committees must conduct their investigations thoroughly and administer discipline judiciously. Some organizations, intimidated by the sheer volume of lawsuits in today's litigious society, have abandoned disciplinary codes of ethics in favor of codes that are strictly aspirational and educational and not enforceable through discipline.

NAP and AIP appointed a joint committee in 1999 to draft a code of ethics that would be binding upon the members of both associations. At that time each association had its own code of ethics, and each had its own enforcement mechanisms in place. Many members of the profession held dual membership in both associations, and these members found it confusing and contradictory to be held to two different standards of conduct. For example, one association's code might caution against charging excessively high fees, whereas the other association might caution against underbidding colleagues.

The joint code of ethics was adopted by both AIP and NAP in 2001.[50] This ensures that the standards of conduct are the same for members of either association as well as for those with dual membership. The first section of the code is aspirational and contains a footnote stating that violations of this section are not subject to discipline. The remaining sections are disciplinary and the two associations have adopted documents providing for an ethics committee to enforce these.[51] The code is significant both for what it says and for what it does not say. Some of the key elements of the code (numbered by paragraph) are as follows:

Parliamentarians must "find within our own conscience the touchstone against which to test the extent to which our actions should rise above these established minimum standards." (Preface)

> The preface makes clear that the code's provisions are "minimum standards" and calls on all members to "rise above" these standards in their personal conduct.

A parliamentarian shall "conduct oneself so as to reflect credit on the profession and inspire the confidence, respect, and trust of clients and the public." (1.5)

Though aspirational and not subject to discipline, this sets the overall tone of the code. The importance of the parliamentarian's integrity and public image are critical to gaining the respect and trust of clients.

A parliamentarian shall "avoid attacking the motives of any colleague, and shall refrain from gratuitously making adverse comments about the work, knowledge, fitness, or other qualifying aspect of a colleague." (2.2)

The profession strongly discourages members from public criticism of the work of other parliamentarians. The word "gratuitously," however, is the key to understanding this provision. Situations may arise in which a parliamentarian has no choice but to point out the error of a previous parliamentarian, especially if the present situation requires correction of a previous error in procedure.

The parliamentarian shall "not misrepresent credentials, education, or experience to a client" and shall "refrain from making gratuitously adverse comments about competing applicants." (3.2)

The question of misrepresentation of credentials is directed to members who are not credentialed to practice professionally. There had been reports of some regular members advertising their association membership as being equivalent to credentialing. As always, the profession is strict about not allowing parliamentarians to criticize each other to prospective clients.

The parliamentarian shall "refrain from giving anything of value to anyone for recommending the parliamentarian's services, except for the reasonable cost of advertising and the usual charges of a referral service." (3.3)

This clarifies a point, previously unclear, that the parliamentarian can pay a fee to a referral service that advertised the parliamentarian's services. The practice of kickbacks for recommending services, however, remains unethical.

The parliamentarian shall "decline any appointment in which the parliamentarian is likely to be unduly restricted in the exercise of independent professional judgment." (3.6)

This clarifies that parliamentarians may not accept assignments in which they are given advance directives to work toward the passage or defeat of certain measures. They may not work toward the election or defeat of any candidate for office, or any other predetermined substantive objective.

The parliamentarian shall "advise the client on the proper application of the accepted rules of parliamentary procedure notwithstanding the client's personal desires in the matter." (4.3)

The temptation to tell clients what they want to hear is ever present. The parliamentarian must give the correct advice, even if this will result in termination of employment.

The parliamentarian shall "maintain a position of objectivity and impartiality and refrain from participating in debate." (4.6)

The word "position" is the key to understanding this provision. It is not enough to be impartial and objective; the parliamentarian must also give the appearance of being objective and impartial at all times.

One item that was completely omitted from the code of ethics is the fees that parliamentarians charge for professional services. Although there has been much discussion of fees among professionals, it was decided to allow each member to charge as much or as little as desired. No attempt has been made to standardize fees or to discourage parliamentarians from working pro bono. Professionals, however, are constantly reminded that they must maintain high standards of performance at all times, regardless of the fee charged or not charged. Ethics is not measured by fees. Ethical standards apply to all members of the profession at all times and in all circumstances.

> HIGH STANDARDS OF PERFORMANCE
> MUST BE MAINTAINED AT ALL TIMES
> REGARDLESS OF THE FEE CHARGED.

CHAPTER NINE

Building Block: Legal Parameters

From a parliamentarian's perspective, members of the legal profession may be conveniently divided into three groups. Group One consists of attorneys who are fully credentialed as parliamentarians. Group Two consists of 1 attorneys who know little or nothing about parliamentary procedure, don't pretend to know it, and go about their practice of law. Group Three consists of attorneys who, like members of the second group, know little or nothing about parliamentary procedure, but nevertheless engage in the pseudo practice of the profession as if they were members of Group One.

Needless to say, members of the parliamentary profession have meshed very comfortably with members of the first two groups, which constitute the vast majority of all attorneys. Members of the third group, however, have been a source of concern. Some parliamentarians have learned from experience that almost anyone with legal credentials can sometimes give bad procedural advice that will override the advice of a credentialed parliamentarian.

In fairness, it must be stated that the members of the third group are not restricted to attorneys. It is not uncommon for credentialed parliamentarians to encounter pseudo parliamentarians from all walks of life who give bad procedural advice and convince the organization to act on it. The source of the bad advice could be an influential member of the board of directors, a well known financial contributor, a popular past president, a visiting dignitary, or any other person holding a position of authority or influence. Professional parliamentarians know that their advice is constantly subject to challenge, especially when the advice runs counter to the desires of a powerful incumbent administration. So when bad advice comes from an attorney who is not knowledgeable about procedures, parliamentarians tend to accept it as just one more challenge that must be dealt with.

The relationship between the two professions revolves on the issue of dependency. Certainly the legal profession is not and never has been dependent upon the parliamentary profession. If all organizations were to stop meeting and all parliamentarians were to disappear, the legal profession would continue to prosper. The question is whether the parliamentary profession could survive without the help of attorneys, and the answer to this question is very much in doubt. Attorneys have been much more than mere contributors to the parliamentary profession. Their contributions have actually shaped the profession and brought it to its present stage of development.

From its earliest days, parliamentary procedure has come to us from lawmakers in the English Parliament and the United States Congress. When Henry Robert produced his first *Pocket Manual* in 1876, it was unclear to what extent attorneys would influence the procedures for voluntary societies. At a later stage of development, however, three attorneys—William Evans, Daniel Honemann, and Thomas Balch—emerged as major participants in the writing of the *Newly Revised* editions of *Robert's Rules*. These attorney-parliamentarians have been frequent contributors to journals of parliamentary procedure as well as popular presenters at parliamentary functions. They have also maintained close ties with the parliamentary associations. William Evans served as president of NAP during 1979-1981 and Thomas Balch has, at various times, presented workshops or served as parliamentarian for NAP and AIP.

Attorneys who have made significant contributions to the parliamentary profession through their writings include George S. Hills, Paul Mason, and Howard L. Oleck. A number of other attorneys have appeared in leading roles in the parliamentary profession. The most visible of these have included Hugh Cannon, James Slaughter, and Michael Malamut. These three, all credentialed by both NAP and AIP, have done much to promote the profession and have often clarified the boundaries and linkages between the legal and parliamentary professions.

Hugh Cannon served as parliamentarian for the Democratic National Committee during 1972-1976 and parliamentarian for the National Education Association during 1984-1989. His book *Cannon's Concise Guide to Rules of Order*[52] is widely recognized as a major contribution to the parliamentary profession.

James Slaughter, a prolific writer and frequent presenter at parliamentary gatherings, served as the first president of the American College of Parliamentary Lawyers. Paving the way for future cooperation between the law profession and the parliamentary profession, Slaughter notes that "the ACPL is not intended as a competitor to either AIP or NAP, but as a complement to those organizations." Further, the goal of the ACPL is "that both of the two major parliamentary organizations will work with the College on programming for presentations of a legal nature."[53]

Michael Malamut chairs the joint committee of NAP, AIP, and the Robert's Rules Association for Commentary on the Revised Model Nonprofit Corporation Act. He states that parliamentarians should "be familiar with the procedural provisions of the nonprofit corporation law of the state or states where they do most of their practice." His articles in the *National Parliamentarian* discuss issues of concern to parliamentarians raised by the 1952 and 1988 Model Nonprofit Corporation Acts and provide language for overriding the default provisions of these acts.[54]

Betty Green, writing for the *National Parliamentarian* in 1940, was one of the first to suggest a strong connection between the practice of parliamentary procedure and the law.[55] She suggested that parliamentarians are sometimes in a no win situation, caught between the necessity of giving advice based on *Robert's Rules* and the prohibition against giving legal advice. James Slaughter, in his article "Avoid the Practice of Law,"[56] advises parliamentarians to be cautious about the unauthorized practice of law, particularly when advising public bodies and corporations. Many parliamentarians have now adopted the standard practice of giving advice with the caveat, "I am not an attorney, and I do not give legal advice, but—"

Michael Malamut has further refined this language for parliamentarians who serve nonprofit corporations without the benefit of a retained lawyer to address statutory issues. His recommended language is:

> I am not a lawyer and, therefore, I cannot be certain whether the _____ state nonprofit corporation law or some other statute applies to this organization. Also, I am not trained to be able to interpret the provisions of the law. However, if the nonprofit corporation law applies, you should be aware of the following provisions: _____ . . . . When you make rulings on procedural issues, you may want to take the statutory provisions into account.[57]

Hugh Cannon, in his article "The Objectives are Different,"[58] proposes specific means by which a parliamentarian can work closely with an attorney during meetings. He suggests that the parliamentarian be seated close enough to the attorney so that the two can easily confer. Some parliamentarians have found that such an arrangement is not practical for their needs. The attorney is often seated at a business table on the floor rather than on the dais. In this situation, the services of a runner may be utilized to get messages back and forth between the attorney and the parliamentarian. For example, the parliamentarian who foresees a situation in which the chair will be calling on the attorney for a legal opinion may give a heads-up to the attorney to avoid surprise.

Parliamentarians should never think of themselves as second-class attorneys. Their function is very different from that of an attorney. The parliamentarian is focused on procedural issues and strives to help the organization get through its business as fairly and efficiently as possible. The attorney wants to ensure that the organization does nothing illegal and is constantly preparing to defend the organization from any legal challenge. Cannon states that the parliamentarian and the attorney "can generally divide the work between purely procedural and legal matters by simply discussing the potential issues. In those areas in which there is some overlap, such as the interpretation of procedural bylaws that affect the legal rights of members, the parliamentarian can provide insights and suggestions, and then leave the final decision on any legal advice to the attorney."

Although a parliamentarian's work sometimes borders on legal matters, there is ample evidence to support the view that parliamentarians should go about their work without being too concerned with legal issues. James Slaughter states that he has "never heard or read of an injunction or criminal proceeding brought against a professional parliamentarian as the result of improper legal advice."[59] Cannon has noted that "courts of law have shown a consistent reluctance to intervene in the actions of meetings of private organizations. They do so only in cases of obvious fraud."[60] He also notes that "judges themselves are not that knowledgeable concerning procedure, and they have an instinctive aversion of being pushed into the role of becoming the 'supreme parliamentarian' in a legal battle."[61]

In summary, it is true that the parliamentary profession has a history of linkage with the legal profession, and parliamentarians do need to exercise caution when dealing with legal documents. When practical, they should also cultivate a working relationship with an organization's legal counsel. They should not, however, permit legal issues to distract them from their primary focus on procedures. Whenever possible, any matter that involves possible legal interpretation or advice should be referred to legal counsel. In the absence of legal counsel, the parliamentarian can discretely call attention to statutory provisions, using language that avoids the unauthorized practice of law. In no case should parliamentarians attempt to practice as pseudo attorneys. They have their own purpose and function, which are very different from attorneys, and they should continue to function in the role for which they were trained without distraction. A disciplined approach to professional practice can open the door to increased future cooperation between the parliamentary profession and the legal profession.

PARLIAMENTARIANS SHOULD NEVER
THINK OF THEMSELVES AS
SECOND-CLASS ATTORNEYS.

THEIR FUNCTION IS
VERY DIFFERENT.

CHAPTER TEN

Building Block: Technological Change

During the fifties and sixties this country was often described as a "nation of joiners."[62] The advent of the twenty-first century, however, witnessed a reversal of this trend as the applications of modern technology have resulted in reduced membership for many organizations. Many of the client organizations that we serve are now smaller than they were ten or twenty years ago. The increased use of modern technology as a substitute for face-to-face communication has had an undeniably negative effect on membership growth for most voluntary associations. Reduced membership inevitably restricts the flow of dues and other sources of income. The need for meetings tends to decrease as the membership declines.

As organizations have gradually diminished in size, and sources of income have become more restricted, the demands for cheaper and more convenient communication have increased. The trend away from face-to-face communication toward more impersonal forms of communication that utilize the newer technologies has been described by Patrick Webb in his article, "The Future of Parliamentary Procedure."[63] Webb notes that "parliamentary procedure is based upon one common denominator—the value of human interaction and relationships." He is convinced that the future of parliamentary procedure in the United States is in jeopardy due to the increasing use of technology as a primary means of communication.

NAP's education committee has taken a much more upbeat approach to the changing face of our profession, claiming that the new technologies are an "exciting new aspect of meetings" and that the application of parliamentary knowledge using these technologies "is an adventure that has a strong beginning and will only become more prevalent."[64] The committee asserts that anyone who fails to keep up with the latest technology is missing out on the methods of communication used by the next generation.[65]

The advent of webcams, video conferencing, and other technologies, the committee notes, produce significant savings in both time and money. Technology also facilitates decision making when quick meetings are required to discuss an issue. Such meetings avoid the complications of weather delays, traveling to distant locations, and other scheduling problems.[66]

Far from despairing that parliamentarians may be driven out of business, the committee makes the case that new rules are needed for the new electronic meeting formats, and parliamentarians are well positioned to meet this need. Sample rules, case studies, and a methodology for creating special rules are provided. Anticipating the future growth of technological change, the committee asserts that "e-meetings are here to stay. They will become more prevalent and more sophisticated as time goes on." Aware that some older members of the profession might be intimidated, the committee urges parliamentarians "to experiment, to become flexible, and to be open to the possibilities created by the rapid changes in communications technology and tools."[67]

Articles related to synchronous meetings (Web and videoconferencing, chat rooms, etc.) and asynchronous meetings (e-mail) are already starting to proliferate in both NAP and AIP publications. Procedures for the use of e-mail for providing notice as well as new rules and procedures for electronic meetings now appear in our journals.[68] Tutorials on the uses of the new technologies are commonplace.[69] It is fair to anticipate the continued growth of this body of literature as more parliamentarians begin to experiment with technological change.

The question for the parliamentary profession is not whether technological change will occur, but how fast it will occur. Also, many of us with long-term clients want to know how our work will be affected, if at all. It is impossible to answer for all client organizations, but most long-term clients will probably not expect a radically different level of service in a short time. Organizations tend to fall into a pattern of doing business, and members expect this to continue year after year. Groups accustomed to meeting biennially or annually resist changing the frequency of meetings, and debate on this issue can be intense. Electronic voting systems also are usually introduced only after heated debate. Even when changes are approved and implemented, an organization unhappy with the changes can easily revert to its "old" way of doing business.

The important thing to remember is that you, as a long-term employee of the organization, are a known quantity to the membership. They trust you, or they wouldn't bring you back year after year. In the long run, they will probably implement some new ways of doing business, especially in the area of technology. However, these changes will not come overnight. Organizations are much slower to implement changes than individuals. Through a process of trial and error, they will gradually abandon the old ways of doing business in favor of newer, less costly and more efficient methods of making decisions.

The standard by which the parliamentarian will be judged, then, is not whether you know all the latest technology and can apply it instantly. Rather, your success or failure as a parliamentarian depends on your keeping pace with each individual organization that you serve. All organizations are different, and some will move more quickly than others. When they do move, they are likely to move in very different directions. Some will choose to hold electronic meetings by e-mail, even though this practice is strongly discouraged by *Robert's Rules*.[70] Some will move in the direction of Web conferencing or videoconferencing. Others will retain the traditional convention format but will implement a system of electronic voting. Still others will use e-mail only for the purpose of giving notice.

The professional parliamentarian must be sensitive to the needs of each organization and must be ready to help implement change when change is warranted. Many parliamentarians will have a choice of moving either slightly ahead of the organization's perceived technological changes or moving in lockstep with the changes. Those who choose to move slightly ahead of the curve may engage in board training or teach workshops to prepare the organization for technological change for which a need can be reasonably foreseen. Those who choose to move with the changes can wait until the members sense a need for change and then be ready to help the organization move in the desired direction.

The parliamentarians likely to encounter trouble are the ones who reject all technological change and who are not sensitive to the needs of the organizations they serve. Such parliamentarians, if they exist, should probably resign as soon as it becomes evident that the organization is seeking to move up to technology for which the parliamentarian is completely unprepared. With all the help available from both NAP and AIP, there is no valid excuse for a parliamentarian to refuse to participate in any kind of technological changes.

It should be emphasized that not all parliamentarians are expected to become experts in technological change. You do, however, need to find out, through your research and reading, which forms of technology are available and which of these are most likely to apply to the groups that you serve. Some of your clients may opt to make no changes at all, and you should not attempt to force change on these groups. Others will use only telephone conferences, which have been around for years. However, if you do have an organization that wants to implement a specific form of electronic meeting such as videoconferencing, then you have an obligation either to help implement this change or resign so that a parliamentarian more qualified to handle electronic meetings can do the job.

Few parliamentarians, if any, will have to retire from the profession because of technological change. However, they need to familiarize themselves with the available technology that could be of potential service to their clients. Most importantly, all parliamentarians need to be aware of the procedural needs of each organization that they serve and be prepared to make adjustments as needed.

> NOT ALL PARLIAMENTARIANS ARE
> EXPECTED TO BECOME EXPERTS
> IN TECHNOLOGICAL CHANGE.

CHAPTER ELEVEN

A Changing Profession

Any attempt to forecast future trends is risky and subject to error. Based on what we know about the status of today's parliamentary profession and some developing trends, however, it is possible to hazard some educated guesses about the future of our profession.

In four of the building block areas previously discussed, we may anticipate only limited change. *Robert's Rules* will likely remain the centerpiece of our profession for the foreseeable future. Competing authorities which will likely be introduced from time to time should not be discouraged because they produce new perspectives on the profession as well as creative solutions for some of the emerging procedural problems in today's society. The underlying principles of the profession will not change, although the process of developing new rules will cause some principles to be subordinated to newly dominant principles. The profession's code of ethics will likely be amended from time to time, but the basic parameters and boundaries of acceptable conduct will likely remain unchanged.

The most dramatic changes are occurring in the area of technology, and we may expect a continuation of this phenomenon. New technologies quickly become outdated and are replaced by even newer technologies. This is an area that some older parliamentarians fear because they have difficulty keeping up with the rapid pace of change. If, however, they stay focused on the actual needs of their client organizations, they can likely find ways to accommodate the client's procedural needs with only minimal adaptation to new technology. Parliamentarians who utilize the many resources available to them through NAP and AIP will often be able to anticipate the need for technological change in a client organization and help implement, rather than resist, the necessary changes.

Communication is another area in which the profession may expect at least moderate change. Many organizations are experiencing a need for more sophisticated communication skills. As a result, more and more parliamentarians are incorporating board training and advanced workshops on communication skills into their practice. Many organizations now recognize that skills in mediation may be just as important as knowledge of parliamentary procedure. New forms of governance and decision making are also being promoted by some organizations. An organization that adopts the Carver model of governance cannot be ignored,[71] even if the parliamentarian is personally opposed to this form of governance. The same holds for groups that want to use consensus as a model of decision making.

The demands for change in the areas of technology and communication are almost certain to have a direct impact on the educational functions of the profession. Both NAP and AIP have offered extensive programs of education to their members as well as to the general public, but these have been mostly limited to the teaching of parliamentary procedure. A future question to be addressed is how extensively, if at all, the associations wish to become involved in teaching technological skills and communication skills to their members.

One option would be to limit educational endeavors in these areas to the production and sale of educational materials. Whether education in these areas should be systematically taught and possibly tested as part of the associations' credentialing or continuing education programs is a matter yet to be decided. Another option would be for the associations to partner with another profession or perhaps outsource the production of the needed services. Regardless of which option might be implemented over time, it would be very difficult for the profession to ignore the need for educating its members in these related and rapidly expanding disciplines. It will become increasingly difficult for members whose knowledge is limited to parliamentary procedure to function in our increasingly complex society. An interdisciplinary approach to the preparation of future parliamentarians seems inevitable.

Future parliamentarians, like those of today, must be thoroughly grounded in the principles and rules of parliamentary procedure. It has long been acknowledged that they must be able to read well (for example, to interpret bylaws) and write well (to compose bylaws, rules, opinions, and scripts). Now, however, parliamentarians must also be conversant with advanced technological forms of communication, new models of governance, and untested methods of decision making. The profession cannot hide from tomorrow's changing requirements. It is too late. Tomorrow is here.

The final building block of the profession that requires further exploration is the profession's links to the legal profession. We have seen how the very foundation of the profession is firmly grounded in the history of legal decision making bodies, legal documents, and legal precedents. Much of the literature that circumscribes our profession, including *Robert's Rules*, has been authored or co-authored by attorneys. Our members, in the day-to-day practice of their profession, constantly use the same documents and give advice to the same clients as members of the legal profession. At times we seem to be in competition with the legal profession, although we continue to depend on attorneys to nourish and sustain us. Surely this is a questionable relationship in need of some tender loving care and possible future change.

The role of the parliamentarian has traditionally been cast within the framework of assisting the presiding officer of an assembly. In various ways, the parliamentarian assists the entire assembly in the conduct of business, but the most visible role is that of advisor to the chair. Perhaps the parliamentarian's focus needs to be broadened beyond the traditional boundaries to include advising the attorney, at least in particular circumstances. Hugh Cannon has suggested a number of different ways in which parliamentarians can use their specialized knowledge of parliamentary procedure to work with and assist attorneys.[72] Some examples are:

> If the association attorney will be on the podium during meetings, then additional care should be taken to establish a good working relationship with the attorney prior to the meeting.

> It is helpful if the parliamentarian is seated close enough to the attorney so that the two can easily confer.

> During the debate of any issue that will likely involve legal questions, the parliamentarian will probably be able to alert the attorney when points of information are next in line to be recognized by the Chair; . . .

> In many cases, the (parliamentarian's) opinion should be transmitted through the attorney for the attorney's formal advice and approval.

> Generally, the only safe person (to provide a formal parliamentary opinion) is the president, the executive director, or the association attorney.

Cannon notes that it is especially important for the parliamentarian to defer to the association attorney who is "a full time 'general counsel' who works as a staff member with the organization's leadership day in and day out." This person, Cannon notes, has "a more thorough knowledge of the organization and its leaders."

Parliamentarians have already begun to perform in nontraditional roles linked to the legal profession. Some have found actual employment within the offices of law firms, researching the state nonprofit corporation codes, drafting and interpreting bylaws, responding to clients' questions pertaining to parliamentary procedure, etc. Other non-attorney parliamentarians have begun to function as members of state bars, specializing in mediation or other forms of alternative dispute resolution. One can only surmise what possibilities for greater linkage between the professions may lie ahead.

In all the building block areas that change may occur, change within the profession is gradual, incremental, and often imperceptible. Yet changes do occur over time. It is important for parliamentarians to stay slightly ahead of the curve rather than lag behind. The parliamentarian's response to change should not be resistance, but rather that of assisting implementation in a way that produces positive benefits for the client organization. The profession needs to look down the road and ensure that future parliamentarians will be qualified for the tasks that lie ahead.

> PARLIAMENTARIANS MUST
> STAY AHEAD OF THE CURVE
> RATHER THAN LAG BEHIND.

Chapter Twelve

The Parliamentarian of Tomorrow

Many years had passed since Fred first joined the parliamentary profession. He was now a retiree but continued his practice with several groups that had been clients of his for fifteen years or more. At times, he became a little melancholy. He still enjoyed his parliamentary work, but it didn't seem to be going anywhere. None of his groups needed a major bylaw revision or any special help with meeting procedures. Things were going smoothly, perhaps a bit too smoothly. Fred wondered about the future of his profession. Would it fade away? He wasn't sure if there were many client organizations out there still looking for a parliamentarian. Was his life's work becoming a lost art? Would parliamentary procedure eventually become extinct?

Reflecting on his past achievements, Fred knew that his clients valued his work. He rarely met a client that didn't want him back for a return engagement. Some of his clients had retained him for twenty to thirty years. Fred sometimes wondered how his clients knew about him. He had worked mostly behind the scenes while maintaining a low profile. He was almost invisible to the membership except when called on to answer specific questions. Yet the membership seemed appreciative of Fred's services. In fact, he was almost a celebrity in some organizations. How did they know? Why did they keep inviting him back?

At the same time that Fred asked the question, he knew the answer. Fred was popular not so much for what occurred at meetings, but for all the things that didn't happen—things that could disrupt a meeting and cause confusion. Some clients remembered how chaotic their meetings were before Fred was hired. Many belonged to other organizations where, lacking a parliamentarian, the meetings descended into chaos. They could sense Fred's determination that this would *not* happen on his watch. They could also observe Fred's absolute impartiality. Fred could be just as tough correcting an error of the presiding officer or the executive director as he was when dealing with an obstructive motion from the back row.

Fred remembered the time that he had been interviewed for a new job after listening to a tape recording of a recent convention. On the tape, members were badgering the chair with multiple points of order, objections, and points of information. The interviewers asked one key question: How would Fred have handled it? They liked his answer and Fred was hired—for the next twenty years.

One year Fred was unable to attend, so he hired a substitute. The substitute had a family emergency, and she brought in another substitute without telling Fred. Several months later, Fred heard about the confusion on the dais. A delegate had moved an unscripted motion. Everyone turned to the parliamentarian—who wasn't prepared and didn't have a clue. The delegates never forgot that moment, and Fred was virtually assured of a lifetime job. Some of the presiding officers would joke that if Fred couldn't come, they would cancel the convention.

Fred had seen similar scenarios play out in many of his other organizations. Clients noted that even their most outspoken troublemakers tended to settle down when Fred entered the room. Members who had experienced even one really ugly meeting knew that they needed a "Fred" to help keep things in order. They didn't expect Fred to work miracles, entertain them, or be the life of the party. They only wanted an orderly meeting where they could get through their agenda without distraction. Fred knew what his clients wanted, and he sometimes characterized his work as providing "boring" meetings where things get done.

Now, in the twilight of his career, Fred wondered about the future of his profession. He had enjoyed his work, and he knew that his clients were satisfied. But being a parliamentarian was not a very glamorous lifestyle. He worried about how to sell the life of a parliamentarian to young people. First, he would have to find someone interested in meeting procedures. Then, he needed a patient person. Being a parliamentarian does not bring instant gratification. Yes, hard work and perseverance would eventually be recognized, but could a younger person wait for this? Could members of the "now generation" ever accept the subdued lifestyle of a parliamentarian? Fred had his doubts.

Fred's grandson had started coming around lately, nosing through his library. The boy seemed strangely attracted to Fred's collection of parliamentary books and had started asking questions. Who wrote *Robert's Rules*? Why were rules important? Freddie was now in the eighth grade, and he had been elected president of his class. He had his own gavel, and he seemed attracted to business meetings. Grandpa was pleased. He knew that presiding was an important step on the way to becoming a parliamentarian.

Freddie had a big meeting coming up tomorrow, and he asked Grandpa Fred if he would like to sit in. Grandpa jumped at the opportunity. Here was a chance to see his grandson in action. If Freddie could actually preside and keep control of the meeting, maybe there was hope. What's to lose? Maybe he could even get acquainted with a few of Freddie's friends. So the next day, Grandpa got up from his nap and headed for the school where he knew the after-school activities would begin at 3:00 p.m. He got turned around a couple of times, but after asking for directions, he finally found his way to the meeting room.

The meeting room hit Grandpa in the face! A designated chair was waiting for him with his name tag on it, a set of bylaws, and an agenda for the meeting. Freddie was already up front at the podium, gavel in hand, waiting for the correct time to call the meeting to order. Every chair in the room was occupied, and every student had a laptop.

Freddie called the meeting to order, and they went through the pledge to the flag and other opening ceremonies. Grandpa Fred soon realized that this was not an ordinary business meeting. He wished that his client organizations were as well prepared as this eighth grade class. Reports were well written and crisply presented. Motions were written on motion forms in advance. Speakers came prepared to state their views concisely.

As Fred looked around, he saw some telltale signs of advance preparation. Who was that boy sitting up front next to Freddie? Was that a parliamentarian? And what were those papers that Freddie kept shuffling around? Was that a script? Yes, indeed! Freddie had recognized the important role of parliamentary procedure in running meetings. He had appointed a classmate to study meeting procedures, and Freddie and his new parliamentarian had collaborated to produce a script. Nothing was left to chance.

As the meeting progressed, Fred began to see how his grandson was using certain building blocks of the profession. He listened intently as Freddie outlined plans for a workshop on meeting procedures for new members. Aha! Education! While listening to the announcements, Fred fumbled with the books beneath his desk and pulled out a familiar-looking volume. Aha! *Robert's Rules!* As he thumbed through his copy of the bylaws, Fred noticed an attachment that he hadn't seen before. It appeared to be a list of rules of conduct based on the Boy Scout oath that every Boy Scout knows by heart. Aha! Ethics! Fred could almost see the familiar building blocks falling into place, one by one.

Then, something happened that was not so familiar. In the middle of the meeting, one of the student's laptops malfunctioned. Freddie calmly walked to the boy's desk, fixed the computer, and returned to his podium. Grandpa recognized this as the final building block that he had been struggling with. Freddie had been raised on technology, and now he would use it in a way the Grandpa never could. He knew all about videoconferencing, blogs, and Facebook. He used a laptop in practically all his classes. When he wasn't doing homework, he was on his cell phone to his buddies. He was pretty good at twittering too.

As the meeting progressed, Fred reflected on his life as a parliamentarian and the building blocks of his profession. Watching his grandson Freddie, he suddenly realized that his life's work was now passing to another generation. His grandson would be The Parliamentarian of Tomorrow.

WITH THE BUILDING BLOCKS IN PLACE,
THE PROFESSION PASSES TO
A NEW GENERATION.

Appendix A

The Parliamentarian's Job Description

Beginners just entering the profession may wonder how a parliamentarian's time is divided among the many tasks that must be performed. Since each job is different, there is no single answer to this question. In general, however, the professional parliamentarian may expect to spend considerable time in each of the following four areas.

Travel

It would be nice to confine one's work to a local convention center and simply make oneself available to the various groups that travel to the site. In real life, however, this rarely happens. Parliamentarians can expect to be flown to distant locations, most of them near large convention centers. Expect to spend a couple of days packing books, papers, and documents as well as personal belongings prior to each trip; and another day will be required to unpack. Allow two or three hours to unpack in your hotel room and another hour to get registered. You may need to tour the meeting site to find out distances and estimate the time that you will need to get from one meeting to another. You will also need to allow time to file receipts and prepare travel vouchers for reimbursement. Accurate records are important for tax purposes. Don't skimp on record keeping; you will need all the records available to you when taxes come due.

General Communications

Prepare to spend a great deal of time responding to e-mails, answering phone calls, and opening your mail. Much time is spent communicating with clients and prospective clients, answering their questions, preparing contracts, requesting documents that you need to do your job, arranging for meetings, setting times for telephone conferences, etc. You also need to keep up with a constant stream of communications with your colleagues. Don't underestimate the importance of keeping in communication with all your clients. If you expect to be "in the loop," you need to take the time to respond to all requests and inquiries.

Reading, Research, Study

You need to set aside some quiet time for concentrated reading and study. It may require several hours just to do the research and study for interpreting a provision of the bylaws. You may need time to review some sections of *Robert's Rules* and other authorities. Don't skimp on your quiet time for reading. The material that you absorb today will become the basis of opinions that you render in the future.

Composing, Writing

Parliamentarians spend a great deal of time preparing documents and written materials for clients. They must often help draft bylaw amendments. On rare occasions they must write a new set of bylaws for a client. They may draft motions and write the rationale for a motion. Sometimes they will help draft the official call for a convention. They must be alert to which items require notice and see to it that notice is provided in the proper format. Parliamentarians also spend a great deal of time writing scripts. Preparing a script for a large convention can be extremely time-consuming. Some parliamentarians serve as consultants to designated staff members who do most of the actual writing. Other parliamentarians prefer to do the writing themselves. The script contains every word that will be spoken from the dais, beginning with, "The meeting will come to order." It will contain the names of all guests to be introduced, all awards and honors to be conferred. Do not confuse this with an outline. It contains the actual words to be spoken from the dais. Many scripts will use one color of paper for the president, another color for the secretary, another for the treasurer, etc. There will also be backup scripts to be used only if a certain contingency develops.

Script review sessions may be held with the officers, the executive director, and the parliamentarian present. During the oral reading of the script, pronunciations of names are clarified, and typos are corrected. It is common for portions of scripts to be redrafted while the convention is in progress. Scripts should be kept in large three-hole binders so that defective pages can be easily removed and new pages inserted. During conventions, a great deal of time may be spent in redrafting and perfecting each script prior to its actual use.

Oral Communication

Oral communications, especially for a large convention, should be mostly prepared in advance. The parliamentarian can expect to be engaged in many forms of oral communication, including the job interview, oral communication with the presiding officer during meetings, addressing the assembly to explain complex procedures, meetings with committees, etc.

Special attention should be given to the preparation for workshops. If the group is new to meeting procedures, it is usually a good idea to teach with a scripted mock meeting. You will need scripts for the person assigned to preside and yourself. Speaker cards can be prepared and distributed in advance. I recommend the use of three microphones for scripted mock meetings: one for the presiding officer, one for the instructor, and one located near the center of the room where speakers will come to read from their cards. The instructor's notes should also be carefully prepared in advance. The workshop is your primary means of educating members prior to the actual meeting, so nothing should be left to chance.

Appendix B

The Parliamentarian's Checklist

Most of the parliamentarian's work should be done before the meeting is called to order. Not every item on the following list will apply to every meeting; some apply only to large conventions held in hotel settings or convention settings. The entire list, however, should be checked prior to every meeting to ensure thorough, comprehensive preparation.

1. Initial contacts, documentation

   A. Have I obtained a signed contract, letter of agreement, or other document that clearly states the terms of my employment, including when and how my fee and expenses will be paid?
   B. Have I been provided with all relevant documents, including bylaws, certificate of incorporation, standing rules, recent minute, and meeting agenda?
   C. Do I have contact information (including cell phones and e-mail addresses) for the executive office, the presiding officer, and other key personnel?
   D. Have I studied the governing documents and marked or memorized the sections that will likely be relevant for this meeting?
   E. Have I scheduled a meeting with the presiding officer to review the agenda and discuss the handling of important business to come before the assembly?
   F. Have I suggested the use of scripts as a means of controlling the orderly flow of business?

G. Have I arranged for scripts to be written by staff or allowed time in my own schedule for writing scripts?

H. Have I arranged for a script review session to rehearse and prepare for contingencies?

2. Preparations during the two to three months prior to the meeting

   A. Have I studied the governing documents and minutes of this organization to ensure that I am familiar with their ways of doing business?

   B. Have I reviewed the proposed standing rules, and have I made suggested changes to ensure clarity and fairness?

   C. Have I identified key issues that may become contentious, and have I prepared backup scripts for these?

   D. Have I provided the presiding officer with correct language for processing motions and running the meeting?

   E. Have I had sufficient contacts by telephone, e-mail, etc., to ensure that I am in the loop regarding key issues to come before the assembly?

   F. Have I developed a buddy system with other parliamentarians? Do I have contact information for these, including the best times to reach them?

3. Travel to the meeting site

   A. Have I selected clothing for this meeting that is appropriate, lightweight, and comfortable?

   B. Do I have specific driving or travel instructions on how to get to the meeting site, where to park, etc.?

   C. Do I have everything packed that I will need for this meeting, including books, papers, laptop, etc.?

   D. Have I made travel arrangements to arrive at the meeting site at least one full day before I am expected to participate in any committee meetings, script review session, etc.?

   E. Have I arranged for early check-in and/or check-out, as may be necessary to accommodate the meeting schedule?

4. Premeeting arrangements at the meeting site

   A. Have I checked on physical aspects of the meeting room regarding lighting, availability of water during meetings, access to the dais for members, etc.?

B. Have I checked to ensure that the parliamentarian will be seated next to the presiding officer?

C. If a special microphone is to be used for points of order and other interruptions, does the parliamentarian have a clear line of sight to that microphone?

D. Have I checked the location and availability of the spotter, the timer, runners, and others to ensure that the entire presiding team is prepared and coordinated?

E. Have I developed and explained a system of communicating with the presiding officer during the meeting?

F. If a card system is to be used, have the cards been prepared, and does the presiding officer understand how they will be used?

G. Have I identified which committees or officers are most likely to require my assistance?

H. Have I been properly introduced, or introduced myself, to the officers?

I. Have I briefed the vice president on the responsibilities of the office in the event that the presiding officer vacates the chair?

J. Have I checked to see whether the association attorney will be present at the meeting? If so, do I need to meet with the attorney?

K. Have I met with key committees (bylaws, tellers, credentials, rules, etc.) as necessary?

L. Have I checked on the availability of motion forms? Have I taken steps to ensure that all motions and issues are presented to the membership in language that they will understand?

M. Have I made arrangements to be accessible to the membership to help write motions, answer questions, etc.?

N. Have I checked to ensure that I will have early access to the meeting room?

O. If I am scheduled to teach a workshop, have I checked on the location, handout materials, availability of equipment previously ordered, etc.?

5. Personal Arrangements and Logistics

A. Have I ensured that I have a private room in a quiet location?

B. Have I arranged for my clothing to be cleaned, pressed, and delivered in time for the meeting?

C. Have I located the business office, the site of registration, and other key locations?

D. Have I arranged for some form of instant communication with the presiding officer, the executive director, and other key personnel in case of emergency?

E. Have I picked up all materials (including name tag) relevant to my registration?

F. Have I screened all materials provided to me and discarded those that are irrelevant to my job?

G. Have I carefully organized all books, documents, and papers that I will carry into the meeting?

H. Have I checked on the time required for me to get to and from the meeting site?

Appendix C

Sample Contract

Contract Agreement Between
(Organization) and (Parliamentarian)

This agreement between (organization) and (parliamentarian) provides for parliamentary services at meetings of (organization), professional consultations, and other procedural services for the contract period January 1, (year) through December 31, (year). (Organization) shall pay (parliamentarian) an annual fee of $_____ of which 50 percent shall be payable on July 1, (year), and 50 percent shall be payable on January 1, (year). In addition, (organization) shall pay (parliamentarian)'s actual, reasonable, and necessary expenses incurred in the performance of the duties stated below. Duties covered by this agreement are as follows:

1. Parliamentary services for the annual meeting of (organization) held in the fall of (year).
2. Attendance at a script review session preceding the annual meeting.
3. Attendance at regularly scheduled meetings of the (subgroup) and the (subgroup) that are held in conjunction with the annual meeting.
4. If requested, attendance at one or two meetings of the committee on bylaws.
5. If requested, presentation of one or two workshops conducted within (state).
6. Up to thirty hours of additional service as parliamentary consultant, including parliamentary advice given by telephone, written

parliamentary opinions, work on scripts, bylaws, rules, and other matters of a parliamentary nature.

It is understood that, insofar as is consistent with his/her other professional commitments, (parliamentarian) will give high priority to the concerns of (organization) during the contract period. Prior to accepting any other assignment, he/she will first contact (organization) headquarters to ensure that the new assignment does not conflict with the performance of duties stated above. In the event of illness or other unavoidable hindrance to the performance of duties stated in this agreement, (parliamentarian) agrees to provide a well-qualified substitute parliamentarian acceptable to (organization). The substitute's fee shall be paid by (parliamentarian), with expenses to be paid by (organization).

In the event that additional parliamentary services are requested, in addition to those services stated above, such services shall be separately negotiated and paid for by (organization).

This contract agreement expires on December 31, (year), at which time a new agreement may be negotiated.

signature signature
Parliamentarian Executive Director

Other Works

How to be a Parliamentarian. American Institute of Parliamentarians, 2004.

Presiding: You Can Do It! American Institute of Parliamentarians, 2003.

"Parliamentary Procedure: An Essential Skill," Leadership for Student Activities. National Association of Secondary School Principals: Student Activity Division, October 1997.

Enchiridion of Parliamentary Procedure. National Association of Parliamentarians, 1995. Contributing author.

Readings in Parliamentary Law. American Institute of Parliamentarians, 1992. Contributing author.

"Following Robert's Rules: Parliamentary Procedure for Effective Business Management," Business Credit, September 1988.

Parliamentary Perfect: A Listen-and-Learn Program in the Language of Effective Business Meetings. JMK Parliamentary Services, 1985.

Dr. Bierbaum is a frequent contributor to the Parliamentary Journal (AIP publication) and the National Parliamentarian (NAP publication).

Web site: www.ebierbaum.com

NOTES

1   *Robert's Rules of Order Newly Revised*, 10th ed. (Perseus Publishing, 2000). Subsequent references to *Robert's Rules* refer to the latest edition of this publication.

2   Includes RP, PRP, CP, and CPP; retired members not included. At this writing, NAP and AIP have issued credentials to 647 members. Although the number credentialed in both associations is unknown, the total number of credentialed members is estimated to be between 600 to 625.

3   P. 449.

4   Irvington Publishers, Inc., 1991.

5   Da Capo Press, 2004.

6   www.robertsrules.com

7   http: parliamentarians.org

8   www.aipparl.org

9   *A History of Parliamentary Procedure*, 2nd ed. (Minneapolis, 1974). p. 31.

10   *Nonprofit Corporations, Organizations, and Associations*, 5th ed. (Prentice Hall, 1988), p. 1234.

11   Howard L. Oleck, *Nonprofit Corporations*, p. 1235.

12   Stuart Books, 1982.

13   Thomas Nelson Publishers, 1989.

14   Southern Illinois University Press, 1991, p. xiii.

15   "Evolution in Parliamentary Procedure," by Paul A. Carmack, in *Readings in Parliamentary Procedure*, ed. Haig A. Bosmajian (Harper & Row, 1968), p. 34.

16   2nd ed., (McGraw-Hill, 1966), p. 7.

17   Little, Brown, and Company.

18   The Macmillan Company.

19   Hugo E. Hellman *Parliamentary Procedure*, (The Macmillan Company, 1966), p. 6

20   Hellman, *Parliamentary Procedure*, p. 1.

21   Houghton Mifflin Company

22   Ray E. Keesey, *Modern Parliamentary Procedure* (Houghton Mifflin, 1974), p. 6.

23 Keesey, *Modern Parliamentary Procedure*, p. 21.

24 High Publishers, Pueblo, Colorado.

25 H. W. Farwell, *The Majority Rules*, 2nd ed. (High Publishers, 1980), p. 5.

26 Houghton Mifflin Company.

27 Hugh Cannon, *Cannon's Concise Guide to Rules of Order* (Houghton Mifflin Company, 1992), p. xix.

28 Cannon, *Concise Guide to Rules of Order*, p. xvii.

29 Scarecrow Press, Inc.

30 James Lochrie, *Meeting Procedures* (Scarecrow Press, 2003), p. x.

31 Keesey, *Modern Parliamentary Procedure*, p. 4.

32 Lochrie, *Meeting Procedures*, p. x.

33 Cannon, *Concise Guide to Rules of Order*, p. xviii.

34 Merriam-Webster Online Dictionary, 2010.

35 Ralph C. Smedley, *The Great Peacemaker* (Borden Publishing Company, 1955), pp. 30-31.

36 *Newly Revised*, 10th ed., p. xlvii.

37 *Newly Revised*, 10th ed., pp. 56-57.

38 *Newly Revised*, 10th ed., p. 85.

39 Alice F. Sturgis, *Standard Code of Parliamentary Procedure* (McGraw-Hill, 1950), pp. 3-8.

40 Alice F. Sturgis, *Standard Code of Parliamentary* Procedure, 2nd ed. (McGraw-Hill, 1966), pp. 8-10.

41 George Demeter, *Demeter's Manual of Parliamentary Law and Procedure* Blue Book Ed., (Little, Brown and Company, 1969), p. 5.

42 Hellman, *Parliamentary Procedure*, p. 9; Keesey, *Modern Parliamentary Procedure*, p. 14.

43 Farwell, *The Majority Rules*, pp. 6-7; Lochrie, *Meeting Procedures*, p. 1.

44 John Gilbert Heinberg, "A History of the Majority Principle," in *Readings in Parliamentary Procedure*, ed. Haig A. Bosmajian (Harper & Row, 1968), pp. 91-93.

45 *A History of Parliamentary Procedure*, 2nd ed. (Minneapolis, 1974), p. 14.

46 Lochrie, *Meeting Procedures*, p. 5.

47 Alice F. Sturgis, *Standard Code of Parliamentary Procedure* (McGraw-Hill, 1950), p. 3.

48 Lochrie, *Meeting Procedures*, p. 3.

49 See *Parliamentary Journal*, April, 2006, pp. 43-55.

50 *Parliamentary Journal*, AIP (July, 2002), pp. 88-90; *National Parliamentarian*, NAP (3rd quarter, 2002), pp. 8-9.

51 At this writing, NAP and AIP are negotiating the possibility of a single ethics committee for both associations and a common document for the enforcement of the disciplinary provisions of the code.

52 Houghton Mifflin Company, 1992, 1995, 2001.

53 "New Parliamentary Organization Formed: The American College of Parliamentary Lawyers," *National Parliamentarian*, 1st Q, 2008, pp. 28-29.

54 "Summary of Sources of State Nonprofit Corporation Laws," 2nd Q, 2008, pp. 8-11; "Issues of Concern to Parliamentarians Raised by the 1952 Model Nonprofit Corporation Act," 3rd Q, 2008, pp. 16-21; 4th Q, 2008, pp. 22-29; 4th Q, 2009, pp. 24-31." "Sample Bylaw Provisions for Overriding the Default Provisions of the 2008 Model Nonprofit Corporation Act," 2nd Q, 2009, pp. 5-9; 3rd Q, 2009, pp. 12-18.

55 January, 1940, p. 11.

56 *National Parliamentarian*, 1st Q, 2003, pp. 16-18.

57 "Summary of Sources of State Nonprofit Corporation Law," *National Parliamentarian*, 2nd Q, 2008, p.9.

58 *National Parliamentarian*, 1st Q, 2003, pp. 19-23.

59 *National Parliamentarian*, 1st Q, 2003, p. 18.

60 Cannon, *Concise Guide to Rules of Order*, p. 88.

61 *National Parliamentarian*, 1st Q, 2003, p. 22.

62 Hellman, *Parliamentary Procedure*, p. 4.

63 *National Parliamentarian*, 3rd Q, 2005, pp. 11-12.

64 "Rules for Electronic Meetings," NAP (Educational Resources Committee, 2009), p. 3.

65 P. 49.

66 P. 18.

67 P. 55.

68 "Considerations for the Use of E-mail for Providing Notice," by Robert B. Fish and Roger G. Hanshaw, *National Parliamentarian* (1st Q, 2010), pp. 27-32; "E-Meeting Rules and Procedures Updated for the Real World," by John D. Stackpole, *Parliamentary Journal* (October, 2009), pp. 123-142; "Sample Rules for Synchronous e-Meetings," by Paul McClintock, *PJ*, (October 2009), pp. 143-146.

69 "Tutorial for Internet Chat Room Meetings," *Parliamentary Journal* (October, 2009), pp. 147-149.

70 "Rules for Electronic Meetings," NAP (Educational Resources Committee, 2009), p. 2.

71 *Boards that Make a Difference*, 2nd ed., by John Carver (Josey-Bass Publishers, 1997).

72 "The Objectives are Different," *National Parliamentarian* (1st Q, 2003), pp. 19-23.

www.ingramcontent.com/pod-product-compliance
Lightning Source LLC
Chambersburg PA
CBHW020342290526
45785CB00005B/2141